Seeing it God's Way

Seeing it God's Way

Belinda Mackay

paternoster
Lifestyle

First published in 2001 by Paternoster Lifestyle

07 06 05 04 03 02 01   7 6 5 4 3 2 1

Paternoster Lifestyle is an imprint of Paternoster Publishing,
P.O. Box 300, Carlisle, Cumbria, CA3 0QS, UK
and Paternoster Publishing USA
PO Box 1047, Waynesboro, GA30830-2047
www.paternoster-publishing.com

British Library Cataloguing in Publication Data
A catalogue record for this book is available from the British
Library

ISBN 1-85078-377-2

Cover Design by Campsie
Printed in Great Britain by Cox and Wyman Ltd.
Cardiff Road, Reading, Berkshire, RG1 8EX

Contents

Dedication

This book is dedicated to my father as I greatly appreciated his suggestions and assistance in this project. He collected newspaper cuttings and cleared away the cobwebs of memories from years past to recall significant events and answered my assortment of peculiar questions.

Acknowledgements

I would like to thank the many friends who spurred me on in this endeavour and gave practical assistance. Special thanks to my family for all their practical help producing books and articles and remembering details of events years ago. Also: David Grant and Marty Wytkamp for the Arthur Stace articles and Jacyl Shaw for the Edward Dunlop Awards information.

I appreciated the assistance of Denise King and people from the Royal Australasian College of Surgeons in the compilation of Dr Peter King's story, in particular Colin Smith, archivist, Drs D.G. MacLeish, John Royle, Ian Gunn and Gordon Trinca. For information about Christian Outreach Ministries, thanks go to Keith Greenwood.

Author's notes

When writing about people in situations in China, I used English names. This may be confusing for readers who expect Chinese names. Most of the people I mixed with at the college where I taught English and elsewhere, had English names. This is common in educational institutions throughout China. I have given them new names in the book in order to protect their identities.

Abbreviations used for the states in Australia are:

South Australia SA,
Western Australia WA,
Victoria VIC,
Tasmania TAS,
Queensland QLD,
New South Wales NSW,
Northern Territory NT,
Australian Capital Territory ACT.

Introduction

Some people who have been called to serve in a ministry, have had 'moments' of sudden insight and perception concerning the nature and core of the desperate circumstances of others. They have experienced God's heart, been fired with his compassion and had the courage to say: 'What do you want me to do about this, Lord?' The Lord sets out his master plan to relieve the suffering of the people group he wants to care for through them. The choice to be obedient often weighs heavily on the person but the results far outweigh anything they could have dreamed before the adventure started.

Ken Gire describes such moments as 'windows of the soul' in his book of the same name. My life changed course after such a 'moment' in 1987 in Beijing. On the first day of the holiday my companions and I drove to Tiananmen Square through snow and thousands of cyclists riding carefully on icy roads. The sights I saw that day came back to me when, a few days later, I was ill with food poisoning.

During my illness, the Lord replayed the images in my mind of the people I had seen. He injected into my emotions a taste of their suffering and also let me feel a slice of his heart of compassion towards the Chinese people.

God's heart in mine changed me.

No longer could I just 'play tourist' on the outside looking in. A month later the Lord opened doors for service in China in the form of dancing in concert tours and later in teaching English in a college for an academic year. There have been many occasions particularly when I was living in China when I had 'windows of the soul' kind of experiences. They were so numerous that I wondered what was going to happen during the next simple shopping trip. But, my own life story is but a short story...

This book, however, includes stories of men and women who devoted their lives to the cause the Lord gave them – such was the impact of the initial 'moment' and subsequent guiding moments along the journey.

For example, Albert Schweitzer once saw the statue of General Bruat in Colmar, then a part of Germany, and now a city in France. The statue made a life-changing impression on him. The majesty or achievements of the man himself did not catch his attention but rather one of the figures of lesser significance at the base of the statue – an African. Following other moments of clarity when he saw his life as God saw it he made decisions to serve humanity and travelled to Gabon in Africa to work amongst the people as a medical doctor. His life influenced people on a vast scale both in Africa and on other continents. He died fulfilled in his calling and place of ministry at Lambaréné.

In writing about people who have given sacrificially and worked hard in the service of others, I am not compiling a list of the 'greatest' or the high achievers amongst the ranks of humanitarians. After all, how can we judge the full impact or contribution to humanity anyway? Do we choose 'the one who influenced the largest number of people'? How would we count them? Many great people were only called to influence a small circle of people, not thousands. Only God knows and judges. But I have included men and women, among countless others around the world, who can teach us today about the implications of following Jesus into the scary ministries they were called to. Their stories inspire and encourage us and can be comforting companions when we are faced with obstacles, difficulties, disillusions or just plain slammed doors. It's nice to read that we could be right on track when these things occur: such things happened to the heroes of the faith as well!

I was saddened to see while researching that there is not much literature concerning the achievements of women. Perhaps there is truth in the unsolicited comment by a man who assisted my research: 'Women don't seem to appreciate their achievements at the time but men always want to be recognised for what they have done!'

Some heroes mentioned are well known around the world, so quoting their words may give more revelation than the facts and figures for their lives which would have been covered by other biographers. Many other heroes are perhaps less well known outside their denominations or country. To them I am indebted for their earnestness to get the job done when there was a need, regardless of whether fame, glory or recognition came their way or not.

I have included several Australian (Aussie) heroes, such as the Rev John Flynn, Dr Peter King and British born Caroline Chisholm, who contributed to making my country a safer and more hospitable place in which to live for the people of their era and their heritage lives on. I especially appreciate their callings because I know how severe a taskmaster my country can be, particularly for the early pioneers. But most of the Australians I discussed worked in other countries. For example, Keith Greenwood cares for orphans in India. Mary MacKillop founded an order in Australia then spread the mission to New Zealand.

I encourage readers to 'see' people and situations with minds and eyes open to God directing our attention so that we 'see, hear and feel' what God wants us to do. In essence, we experience a corner of the heart of God when we take the blinkers off our eyes and remove the protective filters around our hearts.

It's a risky business because seeing things God's way leads to prayer and prayer leads to action. The Lord may ask us to become the answer to our own prayers: for the street children of Guangzhou or the homeless youth of Sydney. But if we are not prepared to be part of the solution, we can't take part in the enormous rewards. (Later on we will see God's dreams fulfilled in lives radically changed by the outpouring of his mighty power in their desperate circumstances.) The complexity of problems in our own country as well as in others' homelands often make us reel back into a cocoon mumbling, 'It's too big, I'm too small, I'm closing down till the problems go away.'

As Paul Borthwick encourages us in *A Mind for Missions*:

> We need spiritual glasses; we need to start seeing the world the way God sees it. In Matthew 9:36, we read that Jesus had compassion on the crowds of people because they were 'harassed and helpless, like sheep without a shepherd'. We can safely assume that Jesus' disciples saw the same people with all of their sundry needs. However the difference between Jesus and His disciples is that He saw the people from a spiritual perspective. He saw their spiritual needs, which led to His command to His disciples to pray for the Lord of the Harvest to send out workers. (Matthew 9:38).[1]

In John 4:34 we read:

> *Jesus said to them, 'My food is to do the will of Him who sent Me, and to finish His work.'*

To wholeheartedly be a co-worker in a project with the Lord is to be able to say the same. Albert

Schweitzer could not contemplate an existence which did not have as its driving force a life of service to humanity stemming from grateful thanks for the life of ease, education and opportunity he had been given as a young man.

---

[1] Borthwick, p. 41

1

Feeling with Mind and Soul

Jesus was a man who didn't wear blinkers but saw what was going on in the lives of those around him. Unlike us, he didn't filter out information that upset him deeply but experienced it in all its ugly richness. He saw into the heart of each person and brought to light the intimate needs of people and nations. Zacchaeus wasn't just a short tree-climber; Jesus knew he was also short on relationships with others, God and with himself. Jesus' clarity of vision and response to overcome evil precipitated the greatest world-changing events in the history of humanity.

As followers of Jesus we are urged to put on 'the mind of Christ'. Then the Lord lets us 'see' difficult situations as he sees them, we will feel with mind and soul and ask the dangerous question: 'What Lord do you want me to do about this?' My wish is that we pull aside the filters and see the situations in the world he presents to us, through his eyes, then hear what he is saying to us about it.

Seeing people and situations that God specifically shows us, from his perspective – with his eyes – is
an overwhelming experience that grips our heart to
the extent that we are compelled to do something
about it. We are always able – we have no choice –
but to pray for the circumstances when we recognise
our human limitations and God's omnipotence.

> We must keep from growing callused. It is easy to hear
> about disasters or deaths on the news without feeling a
> twinge of sorrow, much less compassion for those who
> are suffering. Growing as world Christians, however,
> means that we are willing to open ourselves up to God's
> Spirit and ask Him to help us know how to respond to
> what we learn about. None of us has the emotional or
> spiritual capacity to respond to every need we hear
> about, but we must not compensate for that inability by
> taking on an apathetic, 'who cares?' attitude.[1]

Should we pray, give finances or become actively
involved ourselves in this issue? Having taken this
step it is easy to retreat back into our safe havens.
But through the stories of people who saw the
needs of others and set about overcoming them, I
hope to inspire readers not to retreat but to be
actively involved in whatever particular ministry
opportunities God is calling them to.

The market offers an experience in China of an
instance of 'seeing it God's way' – seeing a street
vendor through Jesus' eyes. I found that spiritual
occurrences such as this became frequent intrusions
in my daily routine while I was teaching in China.
The sights, sounds, smells, stories of the city and its

population kept my senses of heart and mind on constant alert. The Lord was sharing with me what he saw and in the process was giving me the precious part of his heart, just as he did on my crucial trip to Beijing in 1987. (That experience is explained later in the chapter.) Such painful memories can rarely be shared with people who have not had similar experiences.

So it was refreshing to read Ken Gire's book *Windows of the Soul* which poetically and clearly captured on paper such heaven-inspired moments. Ken said:

> Parables are pictures that emerge from the jigsaw events of life, however irregular or disconnected they may first appear. 'All happenings, great and small, are parables whereby God speaks,' said Malcolm Muggeridge; 'the art of life is to get the message.' To see all that is offered us at the windows of the soul and to reach out and receive what is offered, this is the art of living... The natural tendency is to analyze such moments of grace, formulize them into principles so the moment can be recreated, and then legalize the principles into codes of conduct as a measure of spirituality. In doing so, we take not only the spontaneity out of our relationship with God but also the vitality. God, though, will not allow Himself to be confined like a genie in a lamp. Neither will He allow Himself to be controlled as a genie is controlled by the holder of the lamp, summoned at the will of the one who knows just where to rub and how often. It is God who opens the window, not us. All we can do is receive, or not receive, what is offered there.[2]

I realised I wasn't the only one who had seen through these heavenly windows. While reading the stories of other notable pioneering Christians, I found they had had equally riveting happenings with God, propelling them into action at the Lord's bidding and keeping them persisting when circumstances turned adverse.

The chapters refer to others in past and present generations who have gone beyond the hours of prayer and anguish of heart, to work out what they can do to change pressing circumstances. God has honoured their labours of love.

Though spectacularly successful heroes of different nationalities are mentioned, the book calls us to be fruitful wherever God has planted us – around the world or around the corner. I define heroes as those who have had the eyes of the heart to 'see' the situation fully as Jesus would see it and have had the courage to 'do exploits'. In other terms, an ordinary person who is called to act within extraordinary circumstances through the power of God.

Mother Theresa and Albert Schweitzer must be included and lesser-known champions as well. Yet to write exclusively about the giants of the faith who have done great exploits can daunt us, instead of inspiring us, into believing that we are not spiritual enough and therefore only marginally useful to the Kingdom. Therefore included are the lives of some ordinary people whose lives prove that God's power is available to everyone.

Heroes mentioned include military and civilian, past and present, famous and unsung in diverse fields of medicine, the arts, education, aviation, orphanages, prayer, warfare; from everyday heroes to important, influential figures. Big picture people and little picture people each have their place. On the pages march people who have influenced the lives of hundreds of thousands as well as those who have been called to impact only a few. Anyone who has worked in ordained ministries can identify with their struggles, failures and final successes. I have also been challenged by the achievements of people who did not necessarily subscribe to the lordship of Jesus.

I mention the work of a number of Australian heroes. While researching their lives I was struck by how 'international' modern Australian history is. White settlement is only a little over two hundred years old and our ties with Britain and other countries were strong. Then along came globalisation, strengthening our connections offshore to an increasing degree.

Caroline Chisholm, 'the emigrant's friend', was born and died in England but in her lifetime, helped tens of thousands of British newcomers to Australia settle and thrive. The Rev John Flynn, founder of AIM (Australian Inland Mission), at one time was the padre for the Smith of Dunesk endowment which originated in Scotland. Flynn was the main instigator of the Flying Doctor Service.

My heroes reveal many qualities such as leadership, organisation, persistence, discipleship and devotion. Of course our prime role model will always be Jesus. Bible passages illustrate his clear vision and immediate responses to people.

My wish in this volume is that readers will decide to throw away their filters and be open enough to the Spirit to accept moments of revelation and run with the consequences – wherever they may lead. If that happens, missionary committees would cease to need recruitment drives for either missionaries or senders! Running with God's direction is the beginning of new adventures. While researching the lives of influential people I found that they all possessed a sense of adventure of some kind or another because they were not happy with maintaining the status quo. They all thought outside the square they lived in and understood connections between people and resources which together would overcome problems.

Sermons remind us of Abraham's obedience in believing God's promises. I am reminded that he obediently fuelled his sense of adventure, though there must have been nights when he looked up towards the heavens and wondered what he was doing when the promises seemed a long time in the coming.

The two sides to the Abrahamic Covenant speak as clearly to us as they did to Abraham.

> Now the Lord had said to Abram: 'Get out of your country, from your kindred and from your father's house, to a land that I will show you. I will make you a great nation; I will bless you and make your name great; and you shall be a blessing. I will bless those who bless you, and I will curse him who curses you; and in you all the families of the earth shall be blessed.' (Gen. 12:1–3)

The top line is 'I will bless'; the bottom line is 'You will be a blessing'. In short, the blessing we receive is intended both for our use and to be shared with others.

The top line refers to receiving. The modern-day application of this covenant for example, would be building up the church, pastoral care, healing meetings, prophecy, deliverance, etc. The bottom line refers to the ends; giving, evangelism to all nations, spiritual warfare, outreach to the community and nations, etc.

There must be balance between giving and receiving. Too much top line produces inward-looking people and churches, too much bottom line produces burn-out and eventually the end of ministries.

In the film version of Little Women we see the outworking of withheld blessing;

Jo: 'Poor aunt, living here all those years alone in this useless old house.'

Mrs March: 'Yes, her blessings became a burden because she couldn't share them. Wouldn't this make a wonderful school?'

Jo: 'School?'

Mrs March: 'What a challenge that would be?'

Like Abraham let us fuel our sense of adventure. My adventurous spirit led me on a holiday where the Lord showed me the big picture – the size of China.

Beijing 1987

Wearing alpine-like gear, borrowed or bought, we played tourist around all the historical sites in Beijing – the Forbidden City, Summer Palace, Beihai Park and elsewhere. The section of the Great Wall of China near Beijing is spectacular, even through a gale blowing snowflakes in your eyes. Standing on a parapet, hanging onto the wall, to stop myself from falling on the slippery snow, I was pleased I was not on sentry-duty in the middle of winter two thousand years ago. During the whole of the 17 days, the mercury did not rise beyond 5°C and many days it hovered around –5°C (maximum). The temperature must have been at most –10°C, the day at the Wall up in the mountains. At such temperatures, feeling 'cold' takes on a whole new meaning from everyday Australian winter 'cold'.

It was easy to see just from the effects of the climate alone, why so many workers tragically perished in the building of the Wall. (Summer temperatures reach 37°C and winter –28°C in Beijing.) How do people grow crops, bring up families and carry out all the everyday activities of life in such a harsh climate? I admired the Chinese tenacity to live and thrive for thousands of years despite such adversities. God showed me though, how fragile their hold on life can be.

We went to Tiananmen Square on our first day. Driving past in heated taxis, we passed people manoeuvring and balancing bicycles on the icy and deadly roads. Weaving in between trucks, cars and horse-drawn drays, were carts pulled by bicycles.

On one sideless cart was a person lying motionless with only a mop of black hair visible above a thick quilt. Was the person sick? Was the man pedalling so laboriously a relative? I wondered how far they had to go before they reached a hospital.

A few days later, the images we had seen on that first day throbbed in my memory like a video-tape on a continuous loop. One night, the others congregated in one of the rooms for a game of cards. I didn't want to play, so stayed in my room. The Lord unexpectedly asked me to pray regularly for China. Easy to do, but dangerous: it could lead in the future to any destination in time and space.

Surprisingly, within half an hour, I was vomiting violently from food poisoning. Now, when I am sick, nothing in the world penetrates my conscious-ness. All I can think about is that I'm sick and sorry for myself! This time was different. During the six hours I was ill my mind was flooded with the vivid sights of what I had seen in Beijing. The Lord also showed me, through mental pictures, what he sees in the hutongs – the back streets with the faceless tenement blocks where the majority of people dwell. He showed me people living in poverty and despair; the difficult conditions exacerbated by extreme temperatures.

I saw the contrast between what happened when I became ill and when the average citizen became ill. I was attended by the hotel doctor and nurse in the comfort of my own warm room. (More serious cases would be treated at the hospital for foreign patients only.) An ailing Chinese person has to rely

on a relative to negotiate the traffic in a risky journey to a general hospital.

As these images burned in my head, God impart-
ed his heart towards the Chinese people into my
spirit. God's heart was yearning to remove their
suffering and give them 'life abundant'. Next morning I was weakened from the effects of the bug, but
a precious share of God's concern was lodged permanently inside me. This impartation of God's
heart for China changed my heart and propelled me
through all the exciting and rough patches of suc-
ceeding years of China involvement.

A month later a friend, tossing me a pamphlet,
said: 'Hey Belinda, do you want to go back to
China?' Silly girl doesn't she know what my bank
balance is?

Nine months later I was on a plane heading back
to China as the dance leader on my first cultural
exchange concert tour. This was the most adventurous experience of my life to date. Fortunately I was
blissfully naive enough *not* to conjecture where the
tour might lead in the coming years. I had forgotten
the prophecy given years ago in Perth, that the Lord
would open the door for me to dance in many,
many places in the world that I couldn't possibly
imagine at the time.[3]

My years of dancing in China were the fulfilment
of a desire to dance on stage which I cherished
when I was little. I dedicated my dancing ability to
the Lord after hearing a sermon about offering our
talents to his service when I was too young to con-
ceive how he could possibly bring it to pass. These
days as a consequence I handle with care the aspi-

rations of other dreamers. I tell them to remember me when they are famous. No seriously, most visions are planted in our hearts by the Lord and need to be nurtured until they grow into reality. God desires to bless us in order for us to be, like Abraham, a blessing to the world.

Fear or Passion

Running with dreams is a very scary business. We fear we may not see those precious ideas realised but we fear that if they become reality – how will we cope? Will the goal be a disappointment after years of puffing and panting towards it? Gloria Kempton dissects our fears and choices.

> We only have two choices – live fearfully or live pas-sionately. If we have never before consciously and deliberately acknowledged this choice, we've chosen fear... We may think we're safe because we've moved to the suburbs, locked our doors and windows, and enrolled our children in private schools. The opposite is true. Fear is a prison of the worst kind, and it robs us of our passion for living... Worst of all, we've missed the whole point of life on this planet. When we choose to use our God-given passion to stay safe, we deny Christ's power for the purpose to which He's called us. We are here to be God's redemptive agents, leading a dark world to the light... We must choose to confront our fear and embrace passion throughout our lives. This is God's intention for us. 'I have come that they may have life, and have it to the full' (John 10:10).

Passion is His intention... The next step is choosing to act on that calling... That is when people either find excuses not to go ahead or they launch forward, amazing others at their transformation and string of accomplishments that materialise for the sake of the kingdom... Once we decide to follow our calling to passionately love our world, whatever that means for each day, opportunities to express our individual gifts and abilities seem to drop into our laps... If we are driven by fear, our actions will produce more fear. But if we are driven by a passionate response to God's calling, our actions will produce redemption in people's lives.[4]

When losing fears and setting out in directions the Lord guides us to, we can expect negative people around us. Pat Mesiti has this timely warning: 'Associate with other dreamers, listen to them, read biographies of great dreamers. Be inspired by those who are doing the abnormal, and choose to be like them.'[5] He sees the stagnating effects on our goals from the reactions of negative people.

Be very careful where you get your advice from. Certain people, even close friends, live in negativity. For them, being negative is the 'norm'. They tend to only see problems, never solutions. They suffer from 'tall poppy syndrome', not wanting others to overtake them or outdo them. So they try to pull you back to their level. Dreamers need to hang around other dreamers. There's a story told of an old Chinese sage who was coming from a city. A young man approached him and asked, 'My good friend, what is the city like where you have come from?' The sage replied by asking the same question: 'What is the city like where you have come from?' The young man described it as a place with dirty old buildings, dirty streets, bad weather and rude, unfriendly people. 'The place you're headed for is much the same,' said the sage. A little while later another young man approached him from the same direction and asked, 'What is the city like where you have come from?' The sage repeated the same question back to him. The young man described a beautiful place with kind, courteous people. 'The place you're headed for is much the same.'[6]

Road to Emmaus

At a recent Easter Sunday service I attended, the minister preached on the events on the road to Emmaus (Lk. 24) and illustrated the message by pictures projected onto a screen. One of the points he made concerned the distance covered by the travellers in the story. I was struck by the fact that the men walked 11 kilometres from Jerusalem to the village of Emmaus. (Biblical maps show two towns called Emmaus with the alternative names of Colonia Amasa and Nicopolis.) They were deep in discussions with the stranger on the road so the distance may not have seemed too demanding. When they arrived, they pressed the stranger to stay with them in Emmaus. When Jesus blessed and broke the bread their eyes were opened.

Astonished by his appearing, they had to tell the others as quickly as possible, so they fled back to Jerusalem – a further 11 kilometres.

Within the same day they walked 22 kilometres!

When I heard that geography lesson, my toes dug into the floor with tiredness or was it vicarious rebellion? In my wardrobe is a dilapidated pair of Reeboks – 'hand me ups' from my niece. Her sister looks askance at them, wondering why I keep them: relics for a museum perhaps? The soles are still intact thank goodness but the stitching is showing signs in some places of giving up the struggle to keep body and sole together. But they have such a history: how could I throw them out considering their long and distinguished career?

They have carried me on three hikes of ten kilometres round trip through the mountains in China, (and the rest of the three tours). I spruce them up for customs officers who regard them with suspicion when I confess I have been in a village. In Australia they have carried me on numerous fund-raising walkathons to raise team money for China trips and an Indian orphanage. I was 'done in' at the end. Not to the point of moaning on the ground (we dancers must perpetuate our reputation for fitness!).

But I was very, very tired.

Soft, springy soles, transporting feet along pleasant undulating bush tracks: treks of 10, 15 and 20 kilometre duration. With a meal beforehand, drinks en route and BBQ at the end, and with the sun still shining down on our efforts.

But Emmaus to Jerusalem – sandals on bare feet, walking on rocky dirt roads, up and down hills. The return journey was at night: I hope there was a full moon. The passage gives an impression of great haste: it doesn't mention they ate anything before leaving to go back to Jerusalem. Twenty-two kilometres is a long way to go on an empty stomach. It's a long hop to go on a full stomach. I know!

What motivated them to undergo a double journey at such haste? Where did they get their abundant energy?

I think their overwhelming amazement at Jesus' presence with them produced an outpouring of exuberant power motivating them to rush back to the other disciples. Living in our time and place we can't fully appreciate their extreme depression and disillusionment. His life and death had enormous political implications for the whole body of believers then suffering under Roman domination. Many saw in Jesus the Messiah and political leader whom they and their forefathers had been yearning to see. But he had died a solitary death like any common criminal. Would there be an equivalent in western history that caused such a degree of defeat to personal and national spirit?

His appearance pulled the pair out of their depths of misery. Here was proof that their ultimate enemy, death, had been defeated. Realisation that their hopes and dreams were not in vain put springs in their steps. It is astounding the amount of physical energy that is released when the mind is finally released from its bondage by fears, depression and every negative thought that has weighed mind, body and spirit in chains, especially for a long time.

I discovered this same principle after attending my first dance workshop after years of suppressing my dancing ability. (I thought that if I couldn't get into the Australian Ballet, so what was the use of training – silly idea.) The Lord blessed the workshop and my dancing beyond all expectations. I realised how much psychological energy I had used to keep dance on the back burner of my mind when, after dancing all afternoon, I came home and ran twice around an oval without stopping. I took the spaniel I was minding for his exercise, and he was puffing and panting all the way home, but I could have done another round.

I see a parallel here with the disciples of Jesus mentioned in this book. What sustained them, what gave them springs in their feet, to continue their callings especially when opposition loomed from every direction? They could see Jesus clearly, what he had done for them personally on the cross and see what he wanted from their lives. They knew their responsibilities before the Lord, were accountable to him and strove to finish the race.

Caroline Chisholm said after she made the anguished decision to follow the Lord's insistence to get involved in immigrants' desperate circumstances that 'from that time, I never ceased in my exertions'. There's a woman carried along with the strength flowing from the power of the Holy Spirit and the power of her convictions. In one sense she knew, like the two men on the road, the resurrection power that could save the needy God had given her. They knew their strength came from the Lord just as he candidly said of himself: 'My food is to do the will of Him who sent Me, and to finish His work' (Jn. 4:34).

Caroline could see the potential for her visions come to fruition within the next few years. Some heroes, however, like ones from the Bible, are called not to see the end results of their work in their own lifetime.

As David Livingstone commented in his diaries: 'Future missionaries will see conversions following every sermon... May they not forget us (the pioneers)... We are working for a glorious future we are not destined to see.'[7]

Like the men, the heroes mentioned here instantly decided that their business in everyday life had to be subservient to the calling the Lord had placed on them. They had to get out to share the good news they had seen with their own eyes. You will read how after making that decision, the Lord progressively blessed their endeavours and accomplished more than they could ever have thought.

We don't read in the Emmaus passage that the men fell in the door and collapsed and died from exhaustion (I thought I would in the walkathons!). Likewise we read about the energy and endurance of these people with callings in difficult ministries.

Often when disillusionment occurs in ministry, the first reaction of the members of the group is to disband. The 'I'm going fishing' mentality sets in. The men had left the other disciples in Jerusalem and were heading away from the scene. Perhaps they had legitimate business in Emmaus, we will never know. However, Jesus must have wanted them to return to the others. He said later on that they (the group) had to wait in Jerusalem until they were filled with the power of the Holy Spirit (Lk.

24:49). By enacting the shepherd's role he was bringing the stray ones back into the flock and at the same time impressing on them the importance of putting God's mission as their first priority in life.

Challenging stuff, isn't it? But the good news is that he puts springs in our feet to accomplish his will, especially when the going gets tough – when our sandalled feet are constantly hitting sharp stones on the way and it seems as though there is only moonlight to show the way. The disciples didn't lose their path on the return journey and neither did the people in the following pages of my book.

> We must seek a manageable impact. Learning about world events can overwhelm and depress us to the point of inaction if we do not carefully focus our efforts. We must pray, entrusting all the needs we know about to the One who is all-powerful. We can also act in a faithful way, in spite of our limitations. We may not be able to affect conflicts that we hear about regarding Libya, but there might be a Muslim student in our community whom we can invite to our home. We may not be able to stop world hunger, but we can fast for a day and send the money we would have spent on food to a hunger relief agency. (See Isaiah 58:7 on the relationship of fasting to the relief of the poor.)[8]

The involvement I have had over the years in outreach at home and abroad has been anything but conventional. I do not fit the usual pattern. 'Is it short-term missions?' Well, not exactly. 'Is it long-term?' Well, it is and it isn't. 'Are you in one style of work or ministry?' Not really, I have worked in several different areas. Sometimes I wish I was a Wycliffe Bible translator because people have a fair idea of what they achieve and they can put their role into one neat sentence. I think perhaps there are many 'missionary-type' people who also cannot be categorised. Some go on short-term mission trips year after year to the same country. Much of their lifestyle at home is geared with that commitment in mind. Is that short-term or long-term involvement? It's both and it isn't either!

Increasingly I see God calling people into his risky schemes which do not fit neatly into the conventional understanding of mission, held so dear by the local church. He has an infinite number of ideas for reaching those not in the kingdom and some of them blur the divisions between mission, preaching the gospel, business openings, education, medicine, development, the arts; performing and visual. Some missionaries find themselves doing many of those things once they are on their mission field. The work of Operation Mobilisation is a prime example of this. The strength of the organisation is its openness to new ideas about stretching the boundaries of spreading the gospel. No wonder it has grown so much in the last forty years.

What this means is that the local church and in particular missionary committees, need to see that God is working in ways that split open the boxes of how 'outreach should happen'. I know firsthand how limited resources for missions are, but I also know that in order to get the commission completed, then willing participants of God's plans and their funding/supporting bodies must run risks of faith. The Lord is sending out to countries more and more pioneers with non-traditional job descriptions that may become even more so over time as they become enmeshed in the problems of the nation. The local church needs to have the courage to firstly, prayerfully consider if the candidate is in the Lord's will and if so, support such ventures, even if they sound hair-brained in the beginning.

The people God calls for pioneering ventures are often lateral thinkers who may not stick within conventional thinking. Conventional thinkers would not necessarily be open to hear God's unconventional ideas so could not be used for his purposes. Was David Livingstone a conventional thinker? Look at what he achieved and realise that he knew he would not see the full implications of his explorations in his lifetime. For such people, living among those who are not like-minded can be a lonely and confusing experience. As Ben Franklin reflected: 'To cease to think creatively is but little different from ceasing to live.'⁹ They need support from people who can also hear the Lord's vision echoed in their life.

The people mentioned in this book are people who were inspired to think 'out of the box' because they saw pressing needs of others and had the courage to say: 'What do you want me to do about it, Lord?'

The Lord is there to inspire and guide us. His life was anything but ordinary for the times he lived in, nor for our times.

'One Solitary Life' (Anon)[10]

*He was born in an obscure village, the child of a peas-
ant woman. He grew up in still another village, where
he worked in a carpenter shop until he was thirty. Then
for three years he was an itinerant preacher.*

He never wrote a book.

He never held an office.

He never had a family or owned a house.

He didn't go to college.

*He never travelled 200 miles from the place where he
was born. He did none of these things one usually associates with greatness.*

He had no credentials but himself.

*He was only 33 when public opinion turned against
him. His friends ran away. He was turned over to his
enemies and went through the mockery of a trial. He
was nailed to a cross between two thieves.*

*When he was dying, his executioners gambled for his
clothing, the only property he had on earth. When he
was dead, he was laid in a borrowed grave through the
pity of a friend.*

*Nineteen centuries have come and gone, and today he is
the central figure of the human race, the leader of
mankind's progress.*

*All the armies that ever marched, all the navies that
ever sailed, all the parliaments that ever sat, all the
kings that ever reigned, put together, have not affected
the life of man on earth as much as that
One Solitary Life.*

1. Borthwick, p. 47
2. Gire, p. 57
3. Mackay, pp. 2–4
4. Kempton, , pp. 30–33
5. Mesiti, pp. 150–1
6. Mesiti, pp. 150–1
7. Livingstone, D., quoted in Fletcher, p. 15
8. Borthwick, p. 47
9. Quoted in Mesiti, p. 183
10. Quoted in Gray, p. 262

Eternity across the Skies

From chalk marks on a pavement to a message seen by 2 billion people, Arthur Stace's legacy bridged the millennia last night. The centrepiece of Sydney's celebrations, marvelled at around the world, was the single word blazoned across the Harbour Bridge: 'Eternity'.[1]

A man who was an alcoholic and a thief, but found the power of God through one word, has become the Sydney man of the millennium.[2]

Inspired by fiery preaching in 1932, Stace wrote the word 'Eternity' it is estimated, over half a million times on the pavements, doorways and buildings of Sydney for over thirty years.

Reports vary about when he was born, either 1884 or 1885 in Balmain or the Redfern slum area in Sydney. His two sisters and two brothers were drunks who divided their time between jail and helping their mother run a brothel in their home. Three times one sister was ordered out of New South Wales. Stace and his siblings slept on hessian bags underneath the house to avoid beatings from their parents. They stole milk and groceries from greengrocers and neighbours to feed themselves. His brothers died as alcoholic derelicts.

Stace claimed that he became a state ward at twelve years old when his parents threw him out. He took up coal mining on the south coast but steady jobs didn't work out for him so he turned to petty thieving. By the time he turned fifteen, he was in jail for drunkenness. Lost in a life of crime in pre-World War One Sydney, he was hooked into racketeering and sly grog shops. He was a lookout or 'cockatoo' for two-up schools (illegal gambling) and also ran illicit alcohol from a Surrey Hills hotel.

History will debate whether Stace joined the war effort in order to escape his circumstances or because despite his background, there was still a streak of decency in him. He volunteered in 1916, joined the 19th Battalion and served in France as a stretcher-bearer and possibly a drummer. He spent time at the AIF headquarters in London before returning to Australia in 1919. He came home gassed and half-blind in one eye. Like so many others, adjustment to Australian life evaded him and he turned to alcohol to numb the pain of injuries and memories. He regressed from beer to gin, to rum and then to methylated spirits that was sold for sixpence a bottle. He returned to his life of crime and rapidly went downhill.

In a court hearing the magistrate challenged him: 'Don't you know I have the power to put you in Long Bay Jail or the power to set you free?'

'Yessir!' Arthur replied but it was the word POWER he remembered.

What he needed was the POWER to beat the drink. He begged the Police to lock him up.

'Give me a chance. I'm no good!' he cried.

Unemployed and penniless, he heard that St Barnabas' Church on Broadway offered food and tea. This was 1930, the time of the Great Depression and others like Arthur were prepared to listen to the 'talk' just to get the sustenance. He was greatly touched by the neat appearance of the Christians' clothes compared with his own.

'Look at them and look at us,' he told another criminal. 'I'm having a go at what they've got.' He fell to his knees and prayed.

'Suddenly I began crying!'[3]

Through the ministry of the Rev Robert Hammond, Arthur gave his heart to the Lord. Hammond took him under his wing. Stace became a regular at church, visiting mental institutions and helping with the homeless and he also got a straight job working as a cleaner.

November 1932 brought him a dramatic experience that was to set the direction of his unusual future ministry. He attended a meeting at the Burton Street Baptist Church Darlinghurst, where the renowned Baptist evangelist John G. Ridley was preaching from the book of Isaiah. In characteristic impassioned form, the Irishman and recipient of the Military Cross from the Great War cried: 'Eternity – what a remarkable, uplifting, glorified word... because there is only one eternity.'

Stace was stunned by his words: 'Eternity, eternity. Oh that I could shout and sound eternity all over the streets of Sydney. You have to meet eternity.

Where will you spend eternity?'[4]

'Oh that I could blaze that word across the skies!'[5]

Arthur said he walked out of the church with the words ringing through his brain. 'Suddenly I began crying and I felt a powerful call to write Eternity. I had a piece of chalk in my pocket and I bent down right there and wrote it. The funny thing is that before, I could hardly spell my name. I had no schooling and I couldn't spell ETERNITY for a hundred quid but it came out smoothly and in beautiful copperplate script. I couldn't understand it, and I still can't.'[6]

He said he went where God directed him. Up before dawn, he walked the streets to find the places for the Lord's special greeting. This was the first of half a million inscriptions that Stace was to write throughout the suburbs of Glebe, Wynyard, Paddington, Randwick and Central Station. His 'one-word sermons' appeared on walls, seats, roadways and footpaths, preferably in spots where the word would not be scuffed off immediately. His sphere of influence later extended to Newcastle, Wollongong and Campbelltown and country areas until his death in 1967. Though the word would perish in a few days due to pedestrian feet and rain, the meaning would pierce the hearts of passers-by and heaven knows the number who owed their later enlistment into the Kingdom of God, to the commitment of this humble servant.

Arthur's spirit must have daily been pierced by the tension between heaven and earth. Ken Gire expresses this tension so well.

We have a similar mingling of blood within us from
a lineage that is both human and divine. Within us
the dust of the earth and the breath of heaven are
joined in a mysterious union only death can separate.
But that relationship is often a strained one, for while
the body is fitted for a terrestrial environment – with
lungs to breathe air and teeth to chew food and feet to
walk on dirt – the soul is extraterrestrial, fitted for
heaven. It breathes other air, eats other food, walks
other terrain. Most of the time we are burrowed away
in our hobbit holes and don't give a thought to our
heritage.[7]

Jesus said to them, 'My food is to do the will of Him
who sent Me, and to finish His work'. (John 4:34)

For the sake of the unknown thousands who came
into the kingdom because of his obedience, it is just
as well that Arthur let heaven win over earthly con-
siderations.

From the 1930s until the 1960s it [Eternity] appeared
with perplexing regularity. Most people had no idea
where the mysterious writing came from. It seemed to
materialise overnight in most places, its ethereal over-
tones causing some to speculate that it had come from
the hand of God himself. It was only after people
began to notice the neatly dressed elderly man scrawl-
ing his message on the footpath, and after decades of
writing, that his legend spread.[8]

Newspapers mentioned the graffiti and columnists
joined in the community's speculations. Some even

confessed to being 'Mr Eternity' (for the publicity no doubt). When confronted with questions about regulations concerning putting graffiti on the pavement, he responded: 'I've got permission from a higher source.'

He went to a lot of effort at times to chalk the word in prominent places. The only visible 'Eternity' left today is inside the bell in the clock tower of the GPO in Martin's Place – apparently written in 1963.

In 1956 Rev Lisle M. Thompson minister at the Burton Street Baptist Church found Arthur writing with his yellow chalk at the church where Stace was the cleaner and a prayer leader.

'Are you Mr Eternity?' he asked.

'Guilty your honour!' Arthur replied.

Stace was aged fifty-seven when he married Ellen 'Pearl' Dawson, a country girl. His ministry continued unabated until illness slowed his endeavours in the 1960s. He entered a nursing home in 1965. Many missed his distinctive contribution to the suburban landscape when he retired.

In 1967, the Rev John Ridley visited him in the home. He told him: 'Arthur, Jesus is here.' But Stace was already with the Lord.

Two years after his death, Sydney poet Douglas Stewart published the following lines about the night-time artist:

> *That shy mysterious poet Arthur Stace*
> *Whose work was just one single mighty word*
> *Walked in the utmost depths of time and space*
> *And there his word was spoken and he heard*

ETERNITY, ETERNITY, it banged him like a bell
Dulcet from heaven sounding, sombre from hell.

A reminder of Stace's labour is near the Sydney Square fountain. When Sydney architect Ridley Smith designed the Square he wanted to fulfil the witness of Arthur Stace permanently so embedded the word 'Eternity' in silver in stone at the fountain, near the Sydney Town Hall steps. In a strange coincidence, Ridley Smith was named after the evangelist John G. Ridley who had been the catalyst to Arthur's unusual ministry 70 years ago.

The writer of the Sydney Daily Telegraph editorial on 6 January 2000, called for a replica of the sign (the original measured 200 m. by 40 m.) to be permanently displayed in a public space. The message, the writer contended, 'Has given us hope, renewed our faith in ourselves and serves to remind us of the power of one word and its effect on a former alcoholic and petty criminal who was converted by the love of God.'[9]

The power of the moment when Arthur Stace was confronted by the revelation of 'Eternity' all those years before was dramatically revived when the word was illuminated on the Sydney Harbour Bridge on 1 January 2000. Ignatius Jones was one of the producers of the New Year's Eve celebration. He said he wanted to acknowledge Stace's legacy because:

it symbolised for me the madness, mystery and magic of the city. On the one hand, there's the meaning of the word in its temporal sense and on this night of fellow-

ship and good cheer, it shouldn't just be about one
night. This celebration should be eternal in human
life… It says a lot about Sydney that Arthur Stace, who
grew up in a brothel, came back from the war shell-
shocked and [who] became a habitual criminal and an
alcoholic, should be able to reinvent himself and try to
bring joy and meaning into people's lives. This is a
quintessentially Sydney message and one we wanted
to spread.[10]

Unfortunately, Jones didn't acknowledge that God
might have had a hand in the 'reinventing' process.
Certainly the Sydney of Stace's day could not offer
much to a man like him, given the Great Depression
of the thirties and the impact of two world wars.

A Sunny Sunday Afternoon

A group of us had a reunion – we went to church
together for the first time in a number of years.
Missionary callings to India and China and a long
holiday in the USA and elsewhere had split the
group for a year or two. It was good to be together
and I was praising God that through all our wan-
derings, he had kept us safe while away from the
securities of home.

What to do after the service? Donna knew of
restaurants and eateries of all sorts so we headed
for the bustle and colour of people and traffic in a
lively street.

Cafes boasting the cuisine of countless nationalities outdid each other attracting passers-by from

similarly diverse nationalities and sub-cultures. We ate our fill of Lebanese delicacies, then walked to a health shop to buy bottles of freshly squeezed orange juice.

While sucking on our straws, outside the shop, we noticed a girl further down the street standing next to a baby in a stroller. She was yelling at a man who yelled back at her. But her problems didn't start or finish with this troublesome relationship. How much she took in of what he said was anyone's guess. The vehemence in her words and actions, glazed eyes and affected movements suggested drugs were more the issues.

Fed up with not getting anywhere in the shouting match, she turned and pushed the stroller out across the street. We gasped, as she walked neither looking left nor right, straight into the line of traffic. Fortunately the drivers either way were quick enough to stop in time, so the pair reached the other side unharmed.

Only God knew the number of holes shot through by rocks in the young woman's life needing to be healed by his grace and redemption. My heart went out to the baby who was inheriting a life of crying lack.

It is a common enough scene in so many of the cities of the world: the events with local variations are being replayed repeatedly in European, Asian, American or Australian cities and elsewhere every day. The common thread is that the need always outweighs the numbers of people available to join in what God is already doing in each place.

Two of the many people who have worked with people on the fringes of Australian society are the Rev Tim Costello and his wife Merridie. Australian born and bred, trained in education and law and theology in Switzerland, the Lord surprisingly sent them to a completely different environment for their first ministry position. Tim describes their community in his book *Streets of Hope:*

> St Kilda provided the cheapest flat accommodation... it became a magnet for the poorest and most desperate. I found myself constantly asking the question, why is this particular person here?... many were refugees from mainstream Aussie existence... those fleeing broken marriages, middle-class uniformity – or even the law. My legal clients seemed to inclue disproportionate numbers of Kiwis (New Zealanders) and Tasmanians... Some were fleeing repressive regimes, particularly the Russian Jews, East Europeans and Catholic Poles. Bohemian artists, and gays unready to tell family and friends, found refuge... The streets were lined with pawnshops trading cash for broken dreams, New Age bookshops, Jewish trinket stores and lots of opportunity shops. Browsing these sidewalks was a human zoo of wondrous diversity: bikini-clad girls whizzing along and terrifying pedestrians on in-line skates; punks whose purple hair and shaved forelocks raised not even an eyebrow thrashing off to their headbanging music halls of grunge and new-gothic punk; listless druggies with dead eyes just hanging out for a fix... and yuppies in prescription uniform of Country Road clothes, Rolex watch and BMW or Corvette.[11]

His church community ran 'Finding God' exposure weekends which invited groups of six to eight to leave behind their comfort zones and experience other subcultures. The weekend included lunch at the Sacred Heart Mission, visits to Special Accommodation Houses, and a night in a cheap rooming hotel.

> The smells, the sights and sounds always had the profound effect of making people much more aware of the challenge of poverty. We would spend some time in reflection with these groups afterwards and it was often very moving to see the personal growth that people had undergone as they sought to encounter their own fears, prejudices and self-protectiveness. It was always a sacred journey – for God is there in the midst of the mess and brokenness. It just takes time and courage to be there oneself.[12]

Just as Arthur Stace made pedestrians on the footpaths of Sydney stop to consider matters of eternal significance, the work and writings of Tim Costello makes us consider matters about the structures of our society and what we hold dear. Like Stace he blurs the line between sacred and secular. Living and working with those who feel shunned by mainstream society gives him a clearer perspective from the outside looking in. (I like the dedication at the front of his book *Streets of Hope*: 'To all those who shared with us the experience of being committed at the core and open at the edges.') On advertising he comments:

Most parents live with constant internal pressures to buy their children the faddish clothing or toys peddled by advertising traffickers. They are irresistible because their idols like The Spice Girls and soap stars offer their 'friendship' with the product. It provokes a psychic nausea to see the absence of real heroes – and their replacement with airhead media creations who fill magazines like *Dolly*. Advertising is like the ancient Aboriginal practice of throwing the leaves of the corkwood tree into the waterhole and stupefying the fish by the release of its medicinal properties. The fish float to the top, making for an easy catch. We consumers, too, are stupefied by the promises of pleasure in the glittering goodies and are an easy marketing catch. However I do not draw hard boundaries between the sacred and the secular and hope that the discerning reader may recognise the passion for holism… It is this lack of boundaries between Bible and newspaper, prayer and politics that continue to define my worldview and undergirds my passion for life. Indeed, it is only at the intersection of what you think you believe and how you ultimately live that you come to discover what is true faith. Spirituality is the consistent application of one's values.[13]

A magazine asked him what he would like for Christmas. After mentioning he would love to have a big picnic with people from his community on Christmas Day, he commented on Christmas presents:

The best gift has no strings attached. Giving to a reputable overseas aid organisation means making this sort of gift. Although we do learn about the suffering of Third World victims of poverty from TV and from photos in the leaflets about overseas relief received in the mail, we may never know one of these people personally... If I was to give a Christmas present which is focused on the reduction of this level of poverty, I could feel confident that increased literacy and lower fertility will follow. I would be able to dream about the increased abundance of life which may flow to all those who receive the gift I offer, even though I cannot trace its work... in communicating with our God or with the deepest and most private part of ourselves, we may discover that we have made a real gift. It could become the gift of Life and that is what Christmas is all about. This gift of Life is expressed in the sort of life you feel on a picnic, with families thinking back about the patterns of shared Christmases down the years, seeing their offspring warmly relating with adults, talking to their grandparents and sharing stories. That's Life and that's what Christmas is all about.[14]

The Weekend Australian newspaper asked several church leaders to give an Easter 2000 message. Costello responded with the reminder to us: 'We can aspire to more than Olympic gold or economic growth and attempt to be among the most just and egalitarian nations on earth by forgiving the debts owed to us by the poorer nations.'[15]

Tim would have been pleased with the announcement, (recorded in the same newspaper) on Good Friday by our Prime Minister the Hon

John Howard, that Australia will write off $18 million of debts owed by Nicaragua and Ethiopia. This will ease the debt burden of Nicaragua by $5.7 million and Ethiopia by $12.6 million. They are two of the poorest countries in the world. The amounts will be in addition to Australia's foreign aid budget.[16] The news made my Easter because just a few months before my sister and I had signed a petition calling for this kind of response to Third World debt by the wealthier nations. This gesture reminds me of the Isaiah passage:

> *Is this not the fast that I have chosen: To loose the bonds of wickedness, to undo the heavy burdens, to let the oppressed go free, and that you break every yoke? Is it not to share your bread with the hungry, and that you bring to your house the poor who are cast out; when you see the naked, that you cover him, and not hide yourself from your own flesh? (Is. 58:6,7)*

Isaiah then gives assurance and promises:

> *Then your light shall break forth like the morning, your healing shall spring forth speedily, and your righteousness shall go before you; the glory of the Lord shall be your rear guard. Then you shall call, and the Lord will answer; you shall cry, and He will say, 'Here I am'.*
> *(Is. 58:8,9)*

Just as the Australian government's gesture is a sacrifice towards the needy countries, the announcement especially at Easter time, highlights the ultimate sacrifice that Jesus made by dying for us.

The biggest disease today is not leprosy or tuberculosis,
but rather the feeling of being unwanted.
(Mother Theresa)[17]

Daily we are confronted in the media and in our own circle of contacts, with situations that cause us to close off our hearts and compassion because the problems are just too big. We think we can't do anything about them anyway. Who do they think I am, Mother Theresa or someone? We can choose to pull down the blinds.

Tony Campolo describes an experience he had in the very poor country of Haiti:

> During a visit to Haiti, I went to a restaurant. The waiter seated me by a large window. He took my order and then brought me a very attractive dinner. I was about to eat a bite of steak when I happened to look to my left. Eight hungry Haitian children with their noses pressed up against the glass, were staring at my food. I immediately lost my appetite and set my fork down. The waiter, seeing what was happening, quickly moved in and pulled down the venetian blind. He said to me, 'Enjoy your meal. Don't let them bother you.'[18]

I wonder if this was the way Philip felt when confronted with five thousand hungry mouths to feed and the Lord making 'unreasonable demands' of him to think of a solution! When we read John's account of the circumstances, we can sympathise with him. Would we react any differently?

*Then Jesus lifted up His eyes, and seeing a great multi-
tude coming towards Him, He said to Philip, 'Where
shall we buy bread, that these may eat?' But this He
said to test him, for He Himself knew what He would
do. Philip answered Him, 'Two hundred denarii worth
of bread is not sufficient for them, that every one of
them may have a little.' (Jn. 6:5–7)*

Another of his disciples, Andrew, Simon Peter's
brother, spoke up. He at least possessed enough of
Jesus' thinking to offer a minuscule solution.

'There is a lad here who has five barley loaves
and two small fish.' Then traces of Philip's attitude
crept in and blew away his fledgling hope, 'but
what are they among so many?' (Jn. 6:9)

At this point it would be easy to state the obvious: 'It's all too much, there isn't enough food,
money, resources, let's forget the whole idea.'

Jesus, we are told in verse six, already knew
what he was going to do. He was only testing Philip
(and the other disciples). How much faith did they
have? Sheer numbers drowned their enthusiasm to
believe beyond what they could see: remember
there would have been many more thousands of
women and children besides the five thousand men
mentioned in the account.

Jesus must have been disappointed in their
short-sightedness. He wanted them to participate in
what he was going to do to feed the crowd.
Visionaries' efforts are hampered when the people
surrounding them breathe hopelessness into worthy plans and consequently refuse to get involved.
Instead of sensing that Jesus was about to act and

willingly go along with the miracle, they looked at the crowd, looked at the facts and just found a patch of grass to sit on.

Jesus loved giving to people, meeting their needs, and stretched before him over the hills were many thousands of them, probably as far as the eye could see. The story does not say so, but I think Jesus would have felt a mounting excitement because he was about to do something which would please his Father's heart and greatly bless the multitude.

Just prior to this event, Jesus had taught the disciples that his Father had sent him:

> *The Son can do nothing of Himself, but what He sees*
> *the Father do; for whatever He does, the Son also does*
> *in like manner. For the Father loves the Son, and shows*
> *Him all things that he Himself does; and He will show*
> *Him greater works then these, that you may marvel.*
> *And the Father Himself, who sent Me, has testified of*
> *Me. (Jn. 5:19,20,37)*

If the disciples had had hearts which were more open to 'hear' and receive Jesus' teaching and a willingness to know his heart and that of the Father deeply, then they would have picked up on his excitement and asked: 'What are you going to do, Lord? Is it going to be another miracle? Can we help? Tell us!'

The challenge Jesus gives us today is the same. He isn't asking us to produce solutions to the world's problems just by using our own resources and intelligence. He knows better than us how lim-

ited that is! But he wants us to be constantly asking: 'Lord, how are you working in these peoples'
lives, this nation, this situation already and what
are your future plans for them? How do I pray in
accordance with your will?' The big question he is
waiting for us to ask is: 'What do you want me to
do?'

> *But this He said to test him, for He Himself knew what*
> *He would do. (Jn. 6:6)*

God has plans for every individual, people group
and nation and can provide a resolution for every
difficult circumstance. As John said in his closing
testimony:

> *Jesus did many other things as well. If every one of*
> *them were written down, I suppose that even the whole*
> *world would not have room for the books that would be*
> *written. (Jn. 21:25)*

What he wants are Christians who see, hear and feel
his heart to the extent that they will want to actively become co-workers in his plans for the long-
range solutions.

> *Jesus said to them, 'My food is to do the will of Him*
> *who sent Me, and to finish His work.' (Jn. 4:34).*

To wholeheartedly be a co-worker in a project with
the Lord is to be able to say the same. We never
want to have an existence where we are not doing
his will.

[1] Este

[2] Lennon

[3] Ross

[4] Lennon

[5] Thomas

[6] Ross

[7] Gire, p. 48

[8] Lennon

[9] McGovern, p. 21

[10] McGovern, p. 21

[11] Costello, p. 73

[12] Costello, p. 177

[13] Costello, p. ix

[14] Costello, T., 'My Christmas', *The Australian Magazine*, 19-20 December 1998

[15] 'Messages', *The Weekend Australian*, 22-23 April 2000

[16] '$18m Write-off', *The Weekend Australian*, 22-23 April 2000

[17] Quoted in *Observer*, London, 3 October, 1971

[18] Campolo, A. Jr, quoted in Borthwick, p. 154

3

A Second Moses in Bonnet and Shawl

During the season of Lent of that year, I suffered much; but on the Easter Sunday, I was enabled at the altar of our Lord to make an offering of my talents to the God who gave them. I promised to know neither country nor creed but to try to serve all justly and impartially. I resolved in every way to sacrifice my feelings, surrender all comfort, nor in fact consider my own feelings or wishes but wholly devote myself to the work I had in hand. (Caroline Chisholm, Easter Sunday 1841)

If Caroline Chisholm (1808–77) had only known that when she prayed that prayer her decision of obedience would affect tens of thousands directly and many more indirectly, she might have hesitated at the enormity of what the Lord was calling her to do.

Captain James Cook had previously claimed Terra Australis (Southern Land) for Britain in April 1770. When the First Fleet arrived in Sydney Cove in 1788, the ships' company disgorged onto the foreign soil convicts the British government was eager to be rid of.

Warwick Dilley, related to the brother of a Samuel Payton who arrived with the First Fleet, discovered this tragic end to his life in the new colony. To celebrate the birthday of His Majesty King George III on 4 June 1788 the officers were invited to an official dinner by the Governor. Salutes were fired, and 'an allowance of spirits given [so that] on this particular occasion every person in the colony was enabled to drink his Majesty's health. Some of the worst among the convicts availed themselves of the opportunity that was given them in the evening, by the absence of several of the officers and people from their tents and huts, to commit depredations.'

Samuel Payton, a young stonemason who had been convicted at the Old Bailey on 15 January 1783 for stealing a piece of woollen striped cloth was sentenced to transportation for seven years but was subsequently pardoned. Unfortunately this close shave with the law did not stop his tendency to steal. In May 1784 he was indicted before Justice Willes and a jury at the Old Bailey 'for feloniously stealing, on 3d May one watch with gold enamelled case, value £7 and two cornelian seals value £3 the property of William Henry Bunbury Esq. in his dwelling house.' He was sentenced to transportation for seven years.

Accosted by an officer when he was in the tent, Payton was injured and after he recovered, was sentenced to death. Payton wrote a most moving letter to his mother admitting his crimes and pleading the mercy of God on him for the morrow.

He was fifteen years old.

His brother was also hanged in Britain for trivial crimes.[1]

Many had been transported to Australia for minor transgressions by today's standards; stealing silver tablespoons or a loaf of bread. A large number were habitual criminals from the lower middle classes who had been forced into crime through poverty. 'Their crimes written on their foreheads and in their eyes.'

In 1784 a Mary Brenham had stolen two stuffed petticoats, pairs of stays and cotton stockings, cloth, a waistcoat and cap, etc., from her employer. The court records stated she was not yet fourteen years old. A minister of religion made a clemency plea on her mother's behalf. When Mary saw the shores of New South Wales from the decks of the *Lady Penrhyn* she was holding her illegitimate son begot by a sailor. For Mary and most convicts who followed her for the next 80 years, she never left the southern shores. To the motley gathering in 1788 scanning the scenery, the landscape seemed alien and forbidding, and sinister for the convicts who knew they would never see home again. Major Robbie Ross of the First Fleet put into words what most felt: 'Here nature is reversed.'[2]

But strangely there were those who looked upon their foreign home not with dread, but with eager and greedy eyes either because the new land presented scientific inquiry or human possibilities. Caroline Chisholm, later migrating to the settled penal colony of New South Wales in 1838, was of the latter persuasion.

Caroline (nee Jones) was born on 30 May 1808 in Wootton near Northampton, England. Her generous yeoman father and philanthropic mother left Caroline the legacy of their own benevolent natures. As a young girl Caroline constantly visited the elderly and sick in their village with her mother, assisting with domestic tasks in their homes. She attended church regularly and believed strongly in God and her responsibility towards the needs of others. She was always helping neighbours and anyone at all in trouble.

I am fascinated by individuals' life stories in which I can see the Lord's hand in bringing people across their paths in order to make an impact on their lives and to expand their understanding of the world. Their later roles reflected these earlier milestones. For Caroline one childhood experience was to be played out prophetically 26 years in the future when she worked tirelessly to improve conditions for immigrant women and families in the far off colony of Australia.

Her father once brought home a one-legged soldier (one source says a sailor) to convalesce on their farm. History records the divine purpose in this meeting because the man told her stories about far off lands where there were plenty of jobs and enough to eat for everyone. He drew a picture of immigrants in packed over-burdened ships wallowing during long voyages to the remote colony of New South Wales. The tales must have fired the imagination of this seven-year-old because in adulthood she wrote that her first attempt at colonisation was in a pink china washbasin filled with water representing the ocean. She invented a migration game. Using the basin she 'made boats of broadbeans; expended all [her] money in touchwood dolls, removed families, located them in the bedquilt (hills) and sent the boats, filled with wheat, back to their friends'. She remarked that when she accidentally upset the basin with water in it, she was punished and had to continue the game in the dark cellar 'with a rushlight stuck in a tin kettle'.[3]

About this time her father died, tragically leaving her mother to look after a large family. Fortunately the family was left a handsome income. We know from history and a famous painting of her (reproduced on a past $5 note) that she grew into a beautiful woman with blue eyes and flaming red hair. Caroline defended her philanthropic work in the village, believing that her role was her priority in life to the extent that she left many a suitor disappointed in his quest for her hand in marriage. Anyway she was bored with the young men around her who only talked about horses, crops and the weather!

Caroline knew that there was God-given purpose to her life and laid down stipulations about continuing her work unhindered, should she decide to marry. The man who agreed to respect her wishes was an easy-going and scholarly Scot, Captain Archibald Chisholm. Strangely matched with Archibald's expertise on Shakespeare and service as a lieutenant in the East India Company, accounts credit him with keeping his side of the bargain and working unstintingly beside her all their married life. He must have had some considerable influence over her because about the time of their marriage in 1830, she adopted the Roman Catholic faith and renounced her Protestantism. This change later became a hindrance to her involvement in the colony because she was accused of possessing latent Popish intentions along with being resisted in the early days by her fellow Catholics.

Soon after their marriage in 1830 they moved to Madras, India where Archibald had been posted. Her philanthropic leanings found an outlet there. Distressed that daughters of soldiers had little to occupy their days and talents and hence ran wild, she raised two thousand rupees in five days from 'interested gentlemen' to found 'The Female School of Industry for the Daughters of European Soldiers'. It was rather a radical idea even by modern standards because the girls operated the school most successfully by themselves through a number of committees.

Due to Archibald's illness in 1838 the Chisholms sailed to Sydney in New South Wales via Mauritius aboard the *Emerald Isle*. By this time the family had grown with the birth of two sons. The long and arduous journey gave her first-hand experience of the confined and unhygienic conditions on the ships of the day. What the family endured appalled her, but we can see that the Lord through the ordeal was nurturing her spirit to have a heart of compassion for the plight of immigrants arriving in a foreign land with all its dangers.

For the next three years they lived in the peaceful countryside of Windsor west of Sydney before

Archibald was recalled for duty to fight in the Opium Wars in China. Caroline resumed her active life in Sydney. There was much for her to do because conditions in the colony needed drastic changes.

In the eighteenth and nineteenth centuries Australia was seen as a solution to some of the problems in Britain caused by the Industrial Revolution and resultant social upheavals. In the new land wages were high, there were fewer women than men and a chance to build family life. But by the early nineteenth century not many free settlers had arrived. In 1820 the British government sponsored a scheme of assisted passage for immigrants willing to risk a fresh start in the colonies. Men of good character with capital and farming experience were encouraged to apply for assistance. They could look forward to a land grant, livestock and convict labour to work their farm. In 1831 to reduce the imbalance of women to men in the colonies and to solve the female unemployment troubles in England and Ireland, the government paid for single women to migrate. By 1835 settlers were given bounties to bring out immigrants who would work for them as labourers, servants and assistants. But single men outnumbered single women. (In 1821 the ratio of males to females was 100 to 37. In 1841 although the influx of free immigrants had started, the ratio was still 100 to 50.)[4]

Transportation of convicts to New South Wales and assisted passage ceased in 1840. By the next year land prices had risen and jobs were becoming scarce and the boom days had suddenly plummeted into depression. In the same year twenty thousand immigrants arrived hoping for a fresh start. Instead they found that little had been prepared for their arrival and the economic situation was desperate. The immigration system was problematic because the newcomers were bottlenecked in the city where work was scarce but there was no scheme to move them out into country areas where there was a chronic shortage of labour. Men with families and single women from England and Ireland were the worst hit. Used to city life in Dublin or London, they were hesitant to travel inland to the unknown nor did they have skills for working the land.

Summing up the sad consequences of the government's scheme Caoline said: 'The government's immigration system was badly planned and resulted in a great deal of misery among the newly arrived immigrants. Arriving in Sydney the immigrants discovered they were mostly left to fend for themselves.'[5]

Caroline was not alone in thinking that the only way to improve the profile of the colony was to find ways to support the family. They were not offered assistance or protection. Seeing women sleeping in doorways and parks horrified her.

So troubled was she by the plight of the young defenceless girls that she gathered a few to her own cottage and enlisted the assistance of friends to do the same. Her successes in finding employment for a few was little comfort for the hundreds more who needed work and shelter. Wisely she knew that to assist the girls required her whole effort and a large plan on a public scale, not part-time involvement. The task must have weighed heavily on her when she knew she wouldn't be able to devote as much time as she wanted to her own children, given that her husband was still overseas caught up in a war from which he might not return.

Her mind tumbled with the revelation that to help would mean going into the streets and arguing with the brothel procuresses and reclaiming prostitutes. Her actions would bring a storm of protest upon her own and her family's heads. Respectable Victorian society was actively prejudicial towards women acting in public affairs. Only the most courageous (or foolhardy) would risk flouting convention. Caroline didn't want to upset Victorian precepts per se and at heart she was a conservative person. Neither did she want to set up charitable work just to prove her own political theory. She merely wanted to overcome the problems of immigration in the colony. In addition, stacked against her was the stiff opposition to Roman Catholics prevalent in the colony.

As she considered in anguish all these issues, the economic depression was worsening rapidly. The body of unemployed was expanding daily in the streets. She was 'between a rock and a hard place' – her fears on one side and the Lord's persistent calling to her heart, on the other hand the desperation of the immigrants.

Her compassionate heart and the revelations of the implications of her calling propelled her to feel: 'that when any girl abandoned the struggle to find work and fell a prey to the procuresses of the brothels, she herself was "not clear of her sin", because she had not done all she could to prevent it'.[6] That's responsibility. That's knowing and feeling the Lord's heart towards the immigrants to a depth that only one chosen for the difficult task could ever know.

As the opening prayer attests, 1841 was a turning point in her life and ministry. What was needed was a safe dwelling for single women. Her first step was to write to the governor's wife for assistance. Later Caroline recalled: 'From that time, I never ceased in my exertions.' It seemed as the passage asserts: 'No one, having put his hand to the plow, and looking back, is fit for the kingdom of God' (Lk. 9:62). The accomplishments from Caroline's exertions show that she was given the strength never to look back or withdraw to the silence of the bush.

All their public years, the Chisholms insisted that they not draw a salary from their work. This was probably prudent considering the potential for damaging gossip and slander from outsiders if they did so. (Though on a restricted income, the Lord provided for the education of their children in boarding schools in Europe.)

The woman in the black dress with the white collar became a familiar figure at the ships meeting the new arrivals, giving advice to single girls and helping where she could. Though by all accounts the governor's wife later became a member of the committee for the home, Governor George Gipps himself was not immediately won over. This woman urging him to co-operate with her scheme for a hostel startled him. He told friends after the initial meeting that he 'expected to see an old lady in white cap and spectacles, who would have talked to me about my soul. I was amazed when my aide introduced a handsome, stately young woman who proceeded to reason, to question, as if she thought her reason, and experience, worth as much as mine.'[7]

No, I will resist the urge to comment on his overt sexism. But I will point out the obvious, if he had had the 'reason and experience' to know about the conditions the immigrants met in Sydney, he should already have done something to alleviate their suffering, should he not? After all, we learn later in the story that there was a suitable government building left vacant which could have been used. Undaunted by his resistance, Caroline was determined to achieve her goals and prayed even more fervently for guidance. As other heroes of the faith know, when there is tougher testing, there is closer nearness to God.

From the time she offered the prayer at the start of the chapter, she believed she had the divine blessing for the assignment she must complete. Lady Gipps and other significant women of the colony formed a committee. Their names lent respectability to the home although they gave no material assistance. But the consistent resistance of the respectable members of her own Catholic denomination saddened her immensely. They threw 'every possible obstacle in her way and she was daily and hourly requested to give up all thoughts of the Home'.[8] The pressures must have been huge, especially given that she also mothered her own three children, although her husband's small captain's salary extended to some domestic help. (The Chisholms eventually had six children.)

In desperation she decided to spend a few days by herself at Paramatta to think matters through. She missed the boat and went for a stroll instead. Passing Petty's Hotel she found a girl she knew, a beautiful Highlander called Flora. The last time she had seen her was when Flora was living with the other immigrants in tents around the Immigration Barracks. Then, Caroline had tried to warn her about the unhealthy interest a wealthy married man had shown in her. But at the time Flora had not listened to her. Now she was drunk with rum and bent on committing suicide. For an hour Caroline walked trying to comfort her. In the end she found lodgings following her promise that she would not throw herself into the river. The next day Caroline secured her employment as well. The incident had proved to her, better than anything else could have done, that she was right and her critics were wrong. She turned back to the city; from that moment fear left her.[9]

But the end of the tale has a strange twist to it. Some months subsequent to this incident assisted by a boatman, she was struggling to save another young girl trying to kill herself. Caroline offered to pay the man for his help but he refused, saying: 'You do not know me ma'am but I know you and may my arm wither at the socket if I ever take money from you.'

'Why,' she said, 'I have never seen you before. Who are you?'

'I am Flora's cousin,' he replied.[10]

After a few more tussles with the Governor, he gave her a vacant part of the old Immigration Barracks in Bent Street – on condition that the hostel was not to drain one penny of government money. Already in trouble from the Home government over his handling of immigration to the colony, Gipps was not taking chances on the rash dream of a woman.

The 26 October 1841 issue of *The Chronicle* reported that a Female Immigrants' Home was to be opened under the care of Mrs Chisholm. This was none too soon because on 11 September of the same year more than 2500 immigrants had landed on Sydney soil in the previous 17 days. The building was left in an appalling state. To establish 'ownership' of the Barracks she spent the first four nights there alone – except for 13 rats that thought the place was theirs. The second night she spiked some food with arsenic for their party. Her fever at the time and instinct to flee had to be smothered because she would become a laughing stock if she fled at first sight of the rats.

When the home was made ready, it was able to shelter 94 girls on the first night of opening and a few weeks later Mrs Chisholm announced that she had found positions for 735 girls. Her children were still living at their country cottage. Caroline wanted to keep the youngest with her but when a contagious illness spread throughout the hostel, she relinquished them to the care of the nanny. This was an exceedingly heart-rending decision for her to make and yet another sacrifice in a long list for the sake of others.

Caroline set up a registry to assist immigrants find jobs and employers find workers. She knew that the most efficient way to find positions – and quickly – to reduce overcrowding in the home, was to take the girls inland as soon as possible after they landed in the colony.

She sent letters to all settled parts of NSW asking farmers, clergymen, magistrates, etc., to supply accurate information about the types of labour needs. Governor Gipps agreed to send her letters free of charge. (He was getting warmer!) Drays carried produce from farming areas to the city and returned to the country empty. Encouraged by the local press, she gained the co-operation of farmers to use them as transport for immigrants. The first trip failed because the girls refused to go; they were terrified of bushrangers and bunyips. During all her journeys bushrangers (highwaymen) never once attacked them, though there was little point attacking because the passengers would not have had a sizeable purse between them. (Bunyips are mythical animals supposedly inhabiting swamps and lagoons.)

The next day she tried again, this time going along with them. Travelling from farm to farm she placed all 15 women in employment contracts. This set the pattern for the future; she was quickly becoming a conspicuous figure mounted on her white horse 'Captain', leading drays carrying any number up to two hundred people per convoy to farming communities in the hinterland.

The next step was to establish country depots where employers seeking labourers could register their requests, instead of having to make the costly trip to the city. By December 1841 there were depots at Parramatta, Liverpool and Campbelltown and by the end of her first 12 months of operation, depots were established in seven other inland locations – even as far north as Moreton Bay, Brisbane.

Governor Gipps had thawed out by this time. He acknowledged in the Legislative Assembly that if not for her, he could not have informed England that even though the size of the labour supply that poured into the colony was considerable, it had been absorbed without any serious inconvenience. What he really meant was that Caroline's scheme had cost a third of the amount it would have cost the government to implement, and that all the money had come from public rather than government support. Farming communities rallied around the endeavour, providing the travellers with cheap accommodation at inns, often free of charge for Caroline, and food provisions for the passengers as they passed through their districts. (In the bush between towns they all slept under the drays at night.)

Caroline became a legend throughout New South Wales as the following tale illustrates. She was once approached by a formidable bushman.

'Well, Mrs Chisholm,' said he, 'I have been waiting for your coming some time; here's this new-fashioned machine of mine – somehow it won't work.'

She looked it over but was at a loss to know how to get it started either, to the astonishment and indignation of the bushman. He firmly declared that he had heard that she could do anything and yet proved she was 'no cleverer than other people!' After riding back to Sydney she spent time learning how this kind of contraption worked. Three months later she returned in triumph to the man and showed him how to drive it.[11]

Between 1841 and 1843 the colony was wallowing in depression. To help the situation, on four thousand acres of land provided by Captain Robert Towns (after whom Townsville in Queensland is named) Caroline developed a community-farming project at Shellharbour for 23 families.

Caroline was drawn into a case of mistreatment of a girl, Margaret Bolton, aboard the ship *The Carthaginian*. The captain and doctor tied her to the mast and doused her with bucketfuls of icy water, then left her there. Outraged Mrs Chisholm took the men to court, won the case and the pair were imprisoned for six months and fined £50. This test case ushered in stricter controls over conditions on the immigrant ships with which she and her husband were so familiar.

She believed the basic problem with the immigration system was that it did not provide the right kind of people the new country needed. The bounty agents recruited from workhouses and so many of the new settlers were of questionable morality and of little use for the settlements. Arriving also were the 'do-nothing' class of men she dubbed the 'Black-riband Gentry', so called because as soon as they stepped off the ship they bought from the nearest draper black ribbon to hang a spy-glass or dressing-case key with a silver top. They were men quite unfitted to struggling for a living amongst the sturdier colonials. Townsfolk were not experienced farmers and were hesitant to adopt a strange rural existence. Irish immigrants proved to be generally the most easily persuaded to take on the throes of life in the bush. Between 1839 and 1942, 23,705 Irish immigrants came to Australia.

In 1845 Archibald returned from China and the family had to live on a meagre pension. By then the depression had lifted though negative reports about the colony were circulating in Britain. Caroline wanted to present a positive picture to Britain to encourage emigration. So on long, arduous treks throughout the length and breadth of the colony they travelled asking settlers to complete a family history survey. Between six and seven hundred responded and the details were written into her prospectus *Voluntary Information from the People of New South Wales Respecting the Social Condition of the Middle and Working Classes in that Colony.* Smith, Elder & Co., in London published parts of it.

It should be noted that she was hesitant to take on the enormous cost of running the survey and waited until Archibald returned in order to discuss this outlay of family funds. That is significant because after so many years of her being mother and father to their children and having such an active public role besides, she could have side-stepped his opinions, if only out of habit.

The general opinion of the settlers concerning emigration and the pros and cons of living in England versus the colony, was that England was fine for the rich, but Australia was the land of opportunity for the poor. The following year the Chisholms sailed for England in order to convince the British government of ideas about a national colonisation scheme. Before they left, a committee including important notaries of the era who became well-embedded in Australian history, was formed to promote subscription to a fund for the couple. The fund had an upper limit per donor and raised two hundred guineas for a piece of plate as a testimonial of gratitude for her endeavours. Another grateful group was the hordes of bachelors who applied to her for wives. By 1846 hundreds of men were writing to her letters of gratitude for playing matchmaker.

She provided evidence in the House of Lords in England in 1847, claiming to have settled eleven thousand migrants during her brief but eventful years in New South Wales. With evidence at hand, the House of Lords Committee readily accepted her incredible statistics. Looking back over those six years, one can see the snowballing effect of her efforts. It started with the saving of one girl, Flora, from her intentions to suicide. If Caroline had given in to her inclination to give up the idea of assisting the migrants ('The job is just too hard Lord, get someone stronger!') she could not have stood in the House of Lords six years later to give the report of all those appreciative of her compassion.

London's *Punch* called her 'a second Moses in bonnet and shawl'.

Her achievement is all the more remarkable because most of those eleven thousand came through during the depression years of 1841–44.

Unfortunately history does not record the countless numbers of people who, convinced of the worth of the schemes, willingly assisted her. Heaven knows their names though.

Her plans while in England were to promote the colonisation scheme and to re-unite children left behind in England with their families in Australia, and wives with their emancipated convict husbands. She had collated a long list of names of such women and children. While in England she proclaimed the virtues of kindness, sobriety and prayer and championed the role of women to provide stability within families and hence within the wider society.

> If the British Government really wants a well-behaved community to grow up in these Colonies, the social needs of the people must be considered. All the priests and books and teachers you can send, all the churches you can build, will never do much good without 'God's Police' – wives and little children – good and virtuous women.[12]

The plan was based on the notion that hardworking families with small savings could make the best colonists, if only they were assisted to emigrate. She received little support for her scheme, so instead launched her own publicity campaign. She approached London merchants, wrote hundreds of letters and lectured all over Britain about the conditions in Australia.

A new development was the opening of an office for prospective emigrants in London and founding of the Family Colonisation Loan Society. With the aim of helping the poorer class to get to the colony, the Society operated like a bank. Groups of willing emigrants linked to the Society, raised part of their passage money that was then advanced to them in full on condition that it was repaid once they were in Australia. Charles Dickens helped to make the Society a success out of admiration for her work, by advertising the scheme in *Household Words*.

Her efforts paid off when a shift in attitude became common currency. The Empire's dumping ground for prisoners was seen now as the 'working man's paradise'. 'In the eyes of recent migrants the colonies were places where no person was starving, where the dogs destroyed each year more beef and bread than all the poor in Ireland could eat and where the poor man could eat beef and mutton just like a rich man.'[13]

Letters back home from around this time speak of full bellies and a turning from crime. 'Dear mother and father I ham very happy and comfortable, and shud be more so if you was all with us. I never was happy before I came in this beautifule country as I ham now [sic].'

Migrants enjoyed the social mobility that the colony allowed. One wrote: 'Come, men, women, and children, for you can do well here. I am getting good wages … plenty here to eat and drink, and plenty of money. Next year I do intend, if please God spare my life, to go on my own hands [sic].'[14]

The Society chartered its first ship *Slains Castle* that set sail in 1850 with the first 250 excited families. Charles Dickens witnessed the historic sailing.

In her farewell speech Caroline 'begged them not only to be the guardians of the females, but also of religious liberty of their fellow-voyagers.' After tearful blessings, a cheer arose and the last voice cried: 'Three cheers for Mrs. Chisholm's children!' [15]

The following year the Society sent six ships (including one named after her) and Archibald travelled to Adelaide in South Australia to act as the Society's agent. He did not draw a salary for his labour.

The Victorian countryside rang out with the first thrill of gold fever in 1851.

In 1854 Caroline and her children returned to Australia where an overwhelming surprise awaited them in Melbourne. Together the Victorian government and people had raised a colossal £7,500 in recognition of the Chisholms' efforts. (It is interesting that the Victorian and not the New South Wales colonials should rally around them.) In characteristic philanthropic fashion they spent most of the money not on themselves, but on building shelters along roads to the goldfields. Reducing the hardship of the journey enabled families to be united with their husbands and fathers on the fields.

In later life her adopted country had become far more precious to her than her place of birth. However in 1866 the family decided to sail to England, only for a visit they told themselves. But she did not see her beloved land again. Granted a civil service pension of a miserly £100 a year, the couple lived in straitened circumstances for the rest of their lives.

Caroline suffered from a kidney complaint and for five years of her life was so weak, she was confined to bed in a dingy room where she could not see out of a window. After years of seeing the azure skies of Australia this must have been an extra heavy burden. The family later found better accommodation with a bed in a bay window in Fulham where she died on 25 March 1877.

Buried in Northampton, where she spent her childhood, the simple epitaph on her headstone reads: 'The Emigrant's Friend'. Archibald died several months after her. Few newspapers either in Australia or England commented on her death. Feted and honoured while healthy and active, as she deserved, why was there so little fuss made of her passing when the Lord himself would have greeted her with: 'Well done good and faithful servant'? The same fickleness of the crowds in the last days of Jesus' life was alive and well in 1877.

> Her emphasis was always towards building a strong society through stable family life. She challenged the limits under which women were expected to live in order to fulfil her sense of public duty. She truly was the emigrant's friend.[16]

What I find remarkable about the life of Caroline Chisholm was her global or all-encompassing way of thinking. While others in colonial Australia were concentrating on their own farm or other affairs within a small orbit, Caroline was looking at the problems of the whole of the Australian community. In this regard she was similar to the Rev John Flynn, pioneer of the Flying Doctor Service. Caroline saw the interrelatedness of aspects of that community – agriculture, employment, housing, money, singleness, family life, business, migration, etc. She possessed a great understanding of the social difficulties that issued from each of these areas.

Caroline, in seeing the numerous problems also saw how solving problems in one aspect, in turn helped all the others. For example, taking newly arrived immigrants from Sydney to rural farms to work could alleviate the scarcity of labour in the country districts.

Her achievement was made possible by her great gifts of idealism, courage and common sense allied with executive ability and personal charm. Her tolerance was so wide, and her love of humanity so strong that she gave of her best to all who asked her help no matter to what class or creed they belonged. From this love of humanity stemmed her resolve to devote her life without material reward to the service of mankind. She remained steadfast in this resolve through long years when she must often have been wearied and discouraged by criticism and misrepresentation of her motives. Besides her belief in the divine inspiration of her work, and her conviction that she was capable of carrying it out, she possessed another quality which helped to assure success. This was her good-humoured acceptance of the faults and failings of mankind... She knew ... that 'mercenary pursuit is the prevailing passion of man'. She knew, too, when she began her work that she could not expect grateful thanks from all... 'having a very fair knowledge of human nature I knew what I had to expect.'[17]

Her birds-eye view of the issues in Australia and the short-sightedness and errors of the British and Colonial Governments would have been most unusual in women of her day. She was a woman of strong Christian faith so certainly the Lord had been guiding her along the obstacle course of her life. The expansion and development of white settlement owes an incalculable debt to her. Caroline's forthrightness took men by surprise. But for all that, history recorded that she was softly spoken.

> *Do not pray for easy lives; pray to be stronger men*
> *[and women]. Do not pray for tasks equal to your*
> *power; pray for powers equal to your tasks. Then the*
> *doing of your work shall be no miracle, but you shall be*
> *a miracle. (Bishop Phillips Brooks)*

[1] Nagle, pp. 106-110
[2] Keneally, et al., pp. 11, 18, 19
[3] Mackenzie, E., quoted in Kiddle, p. 5
[4] Ralph Mansfield, quoted in Kiddle, p. 9
[5] Flynn, p. 6
[6] Chisholm, C., quoted in Kiddle, p. 13
[7] Quoted in Kiddle, p. 15
[8] Quoted in Kiddle, p. 16
[9] Chisholm, C., quoted in Kiddle, p. 17
[10] Fetherston, p. 98

[11] Mackenzie, E., quoted in
Kiddle, pp. 64-5
[12] Flynn, p. 6
[13] Clark, p. 217
[14] Clark, p. 217
[15] Mackenzie, E., quoted in Kiddle, p. 118
[16] Flynn, pp. 28–9
[17] Chisholm, C., quoted in Kiddle, pp. 186–7

4

Let Us Try

This is not a complete chronological record of Albert and Hélène Schweitzer. Many have done that before me. But among the important events of his long life, I mention a collection of anecdotes which sparked responses in his understanding of himself, his God, European and African societies and his ministry. His expertise covered a number of fields – musicology, theology, writing, peace issues, mission and of course medicine. This chapter will look at just a few of these aspects of his very complex contribution to humanity. His hospital in French Equatorial Africa, now Gabon was on the Ogowe River near the village of Lambaréné which means in the local dialect, 'let us try' – a fitting name for the medical ministry. (Other sources say that the name of the place is actually Adoninalongo which means 'It looks out over the nations'. That in a way is very fitting as well since news of Albert's work at the hospital has been circulated around the world.)

When Albert Schweitzer saw the statue of General Bruat in Colmar, France, what caught his attention was not the majesty or achievements of the man himself but one of the smaller figures at the base – an African slave in chains. The statue which made the life-changing impression on him caused him to comment:

> It is a figure of Herculean proportions, but the face wears an expression of thoughtful sadness which I could not forget, and every time we went to Colmar I tried to find the time to go and look for it. The countenance spoke to me of the misery of the Dark Continent, and even today I make a pilgrimage to it when I am in Colmar.[1]

Schweitzer prayed for the suffering in the world, which was embodied in this statue. He felt even from a young age that his comfortable life was a gift to which he was indebted to society in some vague way. The Lord led him along a path, stopping every so often to give him moments of clarity about the specifics of his future role and philosophy behind his work.

Such thoughts flew in lazy circles in Schweitzer's mind as he was enjoying the cozy solitude of an Easter vacation one spring day in 1886. The ascending sun angled in from a window in his room, as he lay in bed, half-awake, basking in the serenity of early morning. And then, as auspiciously as a sparrow landing on his windowsill, his destiny fluttered into view. 'I awoke with the thought,' he later recounted, 'that my good fortune was not to be taken as something self-evident... In peaceful reflection, while the birds were singing, I decided before I got up that I would be justified in devoting myself until I was thirty to science and art in order to give myself thereafter to direct services to humanity.'[2]

He gained degrees in philosophy, music and theology. For Schweitzer, his first calling came through a window in his childhood, a window he saw in a European town square that looked out over all of Africa. At another window on a spring day in 1886, that calling became clearer. And finally, at a window that opened one autumn day in 1904, it was as clear as the morning sun.

He read an article in a missionary magazine produced by the Paris Missionary Society titled: 'The Needs of the Congo Mission'. The article ended with the words, 'Men who can say, at a sign from the King, "Master, I go forth," that is what the Church needs.'[3]

The search was complete.

His calling was to Africa. He felt compelled to go as a physician. He spent the next nine years getting a doctorate in tropical medicine in Paris. In 1906 he approached the Paris Missionary Society – La Société des Missions Evangéliques chez les Peuples non Chrétiens for acceptance as a medical missionary. In 1913, on Easter Sunday, Albert and his new bride visited Paris then Bordeaux and boarded a steamship to their adoptive continent.

Schweitzer was going to Africa to work, to serve, to heal, to try to pay back something of what the white

races owed the black. But behind that dedication was
also the romantic child, unable to attend his lessons for
dreaming of foreign lands and drawn constantly back
to the great sad figure of the noble black man on
Colmar's Champ de Mars. His whole life had been a
preparation for this moment. Poised between one life
and the next, he looked out at the sunshine and knew
that whatever sacrifices he might have made, whatever happiness he might have left behind, he had made
the right choice. It would have been harder to stay.[4]

It wasn't until 14 April 1913 that they arrived at the
Congo's Cape Lopez and thence to Lambaréné. He
found nothing of the noble savage in the Africans
because the slave traders for centuries had taken
the strongest ones. The coastal tribes had become
slave traders themselves, draining many villages.
Those left were afflicted with smallpox, sleeping
sickness and alien diseases through contact with
whites and natives from other areas. Half the population around Lambaréné died in the first wave of
smallpox. The Fang tribe from the highlands farther
up the river descended and slaughtered the already
weakened people. The white people stopped the
killing and they held the Fangs back approximately
at the location of Lambaréné. But the peace was
uneasy. The missionaries arrived; the first was an
American, Dr Nassau.

When the Schweitzers arrived some time later,
they were staggered by the large number of diseases suffered by the Africans: tropical and
European. In the first year they treated nearly two
thousand patients in the first nine months.

Schweitzer wrote about the frequent operations for strangulated hernia among the Africans that he had to perform. After the patients were freed from pain, he spoke to them and other patients about Jesus who told them to come to the Ogowe:

> The African sun is shining through the coffee bushes into the dark shed, but we, black and white, sit side by side and feel that we know by experience the meaning of the words: 'And all ye are brethren' (Matt. xxiii.8). Would that my generous friends in Europe could come out here and live through one such hour![5]

One of his helpers at the hospital was a man called Joseph Azvawami who could speak several tribal languages as well as French. He couldn't read nor write but learnt to distinguish between the different medicine bottles by the shapes of the letters. Joseph spoke of the parts of the body as a cook would a joint of meat.

'This woman has pains in her upper left cutlet and in her filet. This man has pains in his right leg of mutton.'

Albert had the God-given gift to see matters clearly without filtering out much unpleasant information. He faced things head on. This was a beneficial quality to have in order to cope with the suffering among the Africans. He found the extent of illness there far exceeded his expectations.

> The thing that differentiates Schweitzer is not that he suffered, both in himself and on behalf of other people and creatures, but that the feeling remained fresh and

active in him, where in others it becomes overlaid or
dismissed. And experience with him was remembered
and its lesson learned. This was due partly to the violence of his experiences, partly to the obstinacy with
which he clung to them as something which he knew
to be fundamental and true. Though he learned grad-
ually to be more patient and tactful... experiences
came to him with a vividness that forced him to a decision, from which subsequent events and the argument
of the others had no power to deflect him.[6]

Painful though the traumatic experiences were for
him, especially since he hung onto those feelings,
nonetheless he made right choices in dealing with
such experiences. These choices God used in steer-
ing his later ministry and thinking about the 'reverence for life'. As an adult he wrote: 'I cannot but
have reverence for all that is called life. That is the
beginning and foundation of morality.'

It is so easy for us to make the wrong decisions
after bad situations and become scared and embittered, thus hindering us from being useful in the
kingdom of God.

When Albert was nine years old he started to
blossom as both a Biblical scholar and as an organist. His head was full of a hundred and one questions about the meaning of life and the Bible, which
largely went unanswered by those who supposedly
should have been able to satisfy his enquiring
mind. One day a crucial moment of clarity made
what he had learned become a revelation.

His friend Henry suggested they catapult some
birds. This was a dilemma for Albert because he

knew that killing for sport was a sin. He prayed for
deliverance of the birds but feared mockery from
his friends if he didn't go along with the prank.

> We got close to a tree which was still without any
> leaves, and on which the birds were singing... Then
> stooping like a Red Indian hunter, my companion put
> a bullet in the leather of his catapult and took aim... I
> did the same, though with terrible twinges of con-
> science... At that very moment the church bells began
> to ring, mingling their music with the songs of the
> birds and the sunshine. It was the warning-bell which
> began half an hour before the regular peal-ringing,
> and for me it was a voice from heaven. I shooed the
> birds away... then I fled home. And ever since then,
> when the Passiontide bells ring out to the leafless trees
> and sunshine, I reflect with a rush of grateful emotion,
> how on that day their music drove deep into my heart
> the commandment: Thou shalt not kill. From that day
> onward I took courage to emancipate myself from the
> fear of men, and whenever my inner convictions were
> at stake I let other people's opinions weigh less with
> me than they had done previously. I tried also to
> unlearn my former dread of being laughed at by my
> school-fellows.[7]

There were many lessons learned that day to affect
his heart, mind and spirit. In 1952 he was honoured
by receiving the Nobel Peace Prize, not an honour
that goes to people who tag along with others'
thoughts but to one who is not afraid to air his opinions to the world. (At the hospital in Africa he had
a haven where old, sick animals were cared for. His

special circle of friends were Caramba the dog, Anita the antelope, Parsifal the pelican and Sisi the cat.)

Albert lived through two world wars and knew what the consequences of war meant to individuals and countries. He was born on 14 January 1875 in Kaysersberg in Alsace. Today Alsace is in France but then it was a part of Germany. The effects of the politics of the time forced the Schweitzers into a ridiculous and tragic situation for a few months in 1914. They were living in the heart of Africa, thousands of miles away from the scene of the action, but were penned down under house arrest, forbidden to practice medicine, all because of their nationality.

With much time to write on music and think about the absurdity of war and the preciousness of life, Albert mulled over the question of why people killed and destroyed. While under house arrest he wrote *Philosophy and Civilisation*. He asked why didn't great ideas inspire people? There were more questions than answers. He felt as though he was 'leaning with all my weight against an iron door which would not yield'.

Then an encounter in September 1915 while on a barge trip upriver opened the door to enlightenment. He wrote:

Lost in thought I sat on the deck of the barge, struggling to find the elementary and universal conception of the ethical which I had not discovered in any philosophy. Sheet after sheet I covered with disconnected sentences, merely to keep myself concentrated on the problem. Late on the third day, at the very moment when, at sunset, we were making our way through a herd of hippopotamuses, there flashed upon my mind, unforeseen and unsought, the phrase, 'reverence for life'. The iron door had yielded: the path in the thicket had become visible. Now I had found my way to the idea in which world-and-life-affirmation and ethics are contained side by side![8]

He decided from then on, that he would work for the preservation of life and encouragement of others to open their minds and hearts to do likewise, in order to cure humanity of its tendencies to violence.

(In September that same year, French troops crept up the mountainsides of the Lingen, above Münster and tried to overcome the entrenched German positions on the crest. After thirty thousand men died in the battle, the military situation remained unchanged.)

Albert and Hélène Schweitzer were an outstanding couple of their times. On some issues they carried contrary ideas to those around them. On the question of the value of missions, the common attitude was that missions were a waste of money and that other races should be left undisturbed by the Gospel. (I think the second objection is the excuse for the first.) To this Albert replied:

The first objection... is this: we must leave those races their religion, we must not go to them and take away the beliefs which have kept them happy hitherto, for that does nothing but disturb their spirit. To that I reply: 'For me, a mission does not concern itself pri-

marily or exclusively with religion... It is above all a
task of humanity, which neither our governments nor
our peoples have understood... The only true civilisation consists in living as a disciple of Jesus, for whom
every human being is a person who has a right to our
help and our sacrifice. In short, Missions are nothing
but an expiation for the violence committed far away
by nations that call themselves Christian.'[9]

Because of the geographical position of his homeland, Albert learnt German and French as well as
his native Alsatian dialect. At a dinner party where
he met Hélène Bresslau, she opened the relationship with the comment: 'What gives you the
courage to go into the pulpit every Sunday and
preach in that awful Alsatian dialect? The accent's
ugly and the grammar's dreadful.' Hardly a good
line for catching your man. But Albert must have
seen in her the qualities other girls around him
lacked. Her family were German-Jewish by blood
but her father had broken all association with the
Jewish community and had his children baptised as
Christians.

In her story we can see the Lord preparing a
woman who would be fitted for the rigours of life in
Africa. She had adopted the new emancipation of
women of the era and had a well developed social
conscience. Her methodical and practical mind,
energy, enthusiasm and efficiency were assets for
Albert. She also played the organ. While Albert
learned medicine she trained in nursing having
made the same decision that at age twenty-five she
would devote her life entirely to the service of

humanity. Her deadline arrived a year before Albert's.

The Schweitzer family took to this German-Jewish lady slowly. The younger generation of children dubbed her 'Tante Anstand' – 'Aunt Prim and Proper' as she insisted: 'Sit up straight'; 'wash your hands'. But they saw her beauty and respected her concern for Strasbourg's flea-ridden orphans. In the flow of her dedication, it was natural that she would desire to go to Africa. Her father rightly wanted to see a marriage certificate before they left. Romance doesn't seem to have been a feature of their relationship, rather complementary strengths and weaknesses and like-mindedness on philosophical issues. Nonetheless they were married in 1912.

It is refreshing to see in this relationship that dedication to the cause was the important concern. Rather today, the burning thoughts of young people revolve around: 'Are we meant to get married?', 'Will he/she fulfil my needs?' The calling of God for ministry is often a secondary consideration in the equation instead of holding central place.

Albert and his wife were people of passion who put everything into their role. Hélène was a great help at the hospital. She cared for the instruments, distributed food and drugs, supervised the washing and disinfecting of linen and bandages and a thousand other matters.

They were interned in France during 1917–18 and suffered much illness during their confinement. Surprisingly, their daughter Rhena Fanny Suzanne was born on Albert's forty-fourth birthday in 1919 in Strasbourg.

For health, mental and physical, financial and other reasons, he could not return to Africa until 1924. In the meantime there were requests for organ recitals. An idea came from Söderblom, the Archbishop of Sweden, who suggested he become one of the speakers at the annual series of lectures sponsored by the Olaus-Petri Foundation at the University of Uppsala. He knew that Schweitzer was a defeated man at this time with debts, little money, energy or position to pull himself out of his depression. He knew the fresh air of Sweden would do Schweitzer good. Söderblom was right. Sweden was a good place for Albert to speak his theories to a new audience.

Söderblom suggested that Albert raise some money by playing in a recital tour of organ music in Sweden which was prospering due to the war. The tour from mid-May to the end of June was a great success and he put a huge hole in the debt he owed to the Paris Missionary Society. Refreshed in his mind by the response of the audiences and interest in his life work by Söderblom and others, he set his thoughts one day to return to Africa.

Hélène contracted TB and had to stay behind in Switzerland with Rhena. She wished to return with Albert and thought that she might in a few years when Rhena was older and her own health better. Sadly it was not until 1941 that she made a surprise visit to see Albert in Lambaréné.

By the time Albert made his way finally to Lambaréné he found the jungle had reclaimed much of the land. Many months of labour was required to wrest the clearing back from the jungle.

He and many others built a second hospital and over the years made constant extensions to it. By 1964 the hospital was caring for six hundred patients.

Identifying with Suffering

His words, bright face, his modesty – but most of all his heartwarming sense of humour – moved people everywhere. More and more people called him a 'Prophet in the Wilderness' once they understood his ideals and principles. Many followed him into service in Africa and elsewhere throughout the world.[10]

Awards, honorary degrees came his way. His books became best sellers and inspired millions of people.

Albert died fulfilled in his calling and place of ministry at Lambaréné aged ninety. He had spent his life in close identification with the suffering of humanity. He found expression for his concern in becoming a medical doctor. Intercessors are called to intensive prayer. There are aspects of intercession which are not necessarily found in ordinary prayer. Identification with the sufferer or whoever is in need of prayer, is one of them.

Rees Howells was a Welsh intercessor who lived through the Welsh Revival of 1904 and then through two world wars. He learned through an incident with some orphans that to identify with others' struggles was to be prepared to be the answer to another's prayers.

He had been ministering to a woman who subsequently died of TB. Her husband couldn't or wouldn't cope with their four children and began drinking.

The Lord asked Rees what he should do about the children. The Holy Spirit told him that unless he gave an answer they would have to go to the workhouse. Then the Lord said: 'If anything happened to your brother or sister-in-law, would you allow their children to go there?'

'Certainly I wouldn't,' answered Mr Howells.

'Why do you answer me so quickly about your own fold,' the Lord said, 'yet you have nothing to say about these four little orphans?'

'Well, of course, blood is thicker than water.'

'Yes, but spirit is thicker than blood!'

Eventually the father deserted the children altogether. Howells considered becoming their guardian and he would pay a woman to look after them. But the Lord said to him: 'It is a father they need – not a guardian. I am Father of the fatherless, but I cannot be a Father to them in heaven, so I must be one through you.'[11]

Rees had to face the real possibility that he would have to make a home for the children and care for them until they came of age. This meant 15 or 20 years of putting on hold his hopes and dreams of spreading the gospel throughout the world. He honestly didn't have a paternal love for the little ones so didn't want to take the responsibility on.

But he asked the Lord to change his nature to have a love for them. One night at his bedside, God poured into him his love for the fatherless. He put it this way: 'Any child without parents has a claim on God to be a Father to him, so these four orphans had a claim on the Holy Spirit who was to be a Father to them through me.'[12]

He found someone to look after them for a while as he made preparations to move into his new role. Now it was all joy for him. But on his first day as dad, three sisters of the mother arrived and said that they would care for the children.

Howells had gained through his obedience at the time of testing, the position of 'a father to the orphans'. From that position he could pray most effectively for other orphans and ask the Lord to be the father to them.

---

[1] Schweitzer, A., quoted in Gire, p. 65
[2] Schweitzer, A., quoted in Gire, p. 66
[3] Gire, p. 66
[4] Brabazon, pp. 205–206
[5] Schweitzer, A., quoted in Brabazon, p. 223
[6] Brabazon, p. 33
[7] Schweitzer, A., quoted in Brabazon, p. 39–40.
[8] Schweitzer, A., quoted in Brabazon, p. 242
[9] Sermon preached at the afternoon service at St Nicholas', 6 January 1905 quoted in Brabazon, p.161
[10] Robles, p. 45
[11] Grubb, p. 91
[12] Grubb, p. 92

5

Give a Child a Chance

We ourselves feel that what we are doing is just a drop in the ocean. But if that drop was not in the ocean, I think the ocean would be less because of that missing drop. I do not agree with the big way of doing things.
(Mother Theresa)

If tramping along muddy mountain tracks is good for your fitness, is sleeping on a bunk, minus a mattress, good for your back? Used to my own comfortable bed, I wondered what our accommodation at the Chinese village primary school would be.

'Soft westerner, have your thoughts on higher matters; look at those spectacular mountains, and don't worry about your creature comforts,' I chided myself.

We walked five kilometres from the nearest town to the village through picturesque scenery. 'Picturesque', 'spectacular' and every other inadequate superlative breathed by tourists cruising along the Li River near Guilin could apply equally to these mountains here.

The crags surround us, vast towering eruptions from the valley floor. Each corner revealing a fresh row as if the earth, conjuring them into existence as we went along, was pleased by our exclamations of wonder. Every few minutes a fresh panorama would appear as if seeking recognition in the 'windows' created by neighbouring ones.

Pieces of my Australian culture dropped by the wayside as we slowly entered the world of a minority group and began to understand a little of what their world was like. Tucked away from the bustle of cities and conflicting philosophies, the people are a million miles from what is going on in the rest of the world.

Our team of 16 Aussies endeavoured to make life a bit more comfortable for the 80 boarders who attended the village primary school during the week and could only return home on weekends. We were appalled during our first visit by the conditions of the dormitories. Crowded into small rooms, they slept 'top and tailed' on boards laid across piles of bricks, ten to a bed.

The kitchen was equally dusty. Bricks are heaped up along the once whitewashed walls. The children light fires between the bricks and cook their meals in pots above. I tried to imagine my nieces and nephews in their tender primary years, trudging through highland terrain and all weathers to attend school, carrying a week's supply of food on their backs and cooking it at night.

Subsequent to the first two visits, our tour organiser returned to the village for talks with county officials, the village headman and school principal. They said that the best way we could help was to provide funds for 40 bunks, student desks and teachers' bureaux. Given a tangible request to aim towards, we launched a fund-raising project. Chocolate drives, two dinner concerts, a hike-athon and donations grossed a few thousand dollars: enough to order the furniture from local manufacturers.

So here we were finally back in the village, wondering what they had produced. The village lay tucked between towering pinnacles rising randomly and sharply in every direction from the narrow valley floor. There were the familiar houses built of wood, grey brick and stone with lichen-covered tiled roofs nestling in front of straight rows of vegetables grown in every inch of flat earth.

Children popped out from all directions to see the strange westerners and followed us along the village paths. A red poster with 'Welcorme Australiam Friends' greeted us at the school gate. It was so good to be back at our village – and what a change in the kids! The school was still on holiday, so the boarders weren't in town.

Their first exposure to westerners – ever – was our first visit. At our impromptu concert, the kids had sat silent and anxious, assessing if these aliens from another cosmos were friends or foes. By the end, they had decided we were friendly and followed us noisily 'pied-piper like' along the path out of the village and waved us goodbye. But now curiosity, not fear, drew them out.

I was curious to see the bunks. I spied double metal and wood bunks in a classroom. Somewhat creaky and flimsy for adults they would be fine for lightweight children. That night we slept – carefully – on these bunks in two classrooms. Thin quilts and pillows hired from the hotel in town, softened the wooden beds. Surprisingly, I slept through the unwelcome curiosity of a guest rat that sparked a commotion amongst the other girls.

Two families cooked tasty meals for us in rotund woks over open fires in their almost pitch black homes. We ate on the raised landings outside the houses to the snorts of a disgruntled bull penned somewhere in the darkness under a neighbour's dwelling. I was so pleased he was inside and I was outside.

A hike next day revealed the causes of the acute poverty for these villagers and countless others in the higher altitudes of the uplands. The karst landscape is 'characterised by remarkable surface and underground forms, created as a result of the action of water on permeable limestone'.[1]

As the treachery of the Yellow River (Huang He or 'China's Sorrow') testifies, water cares for no one. Here, rainwater quickly drains away via deep subterranean fissures caused by erosion of the soft limestone. In this area, rain floods the valleys in summer, then rapidly disappears with little rain falling in other months. Consequently, only corn can be cultivated rather than high-yield crops needing greater and more regular rainfall. The precious flat land is also extremely stony. Corn is grown as high as possible up the steep slopes until the gradient defeats the farmers' efforts.

Water storage for domestic and animal use is a problem: women pick their way down dark, slippery steps into deep wells to fill their buckets with water.

Heads peeped round the dormitory doors or silently looked in at the windows. Many more kids were in the school ground. First day of school. The boarders from outlying villages hadn't been told that peculiar *guilos* would be in their classrooms when they returned from holidays. When teachers explained that they would get new bunks, the expressions of amazement were worth a thousand rolls of film. With the team they screwed the remaining bunks together with a determined sense of purpose. Old 'beds' were thrown outside the dormitories. While sweeping the floors the team realised that under the dust was concrete. The dust on the floor and tide mark on the buildings from the flooding bears mute witness to this regular disruption to community life.

'The best part of the tour was seeing some boys sitting on the bunks saying "hen hao, hen hao (very good, very good)!" ' said one of the team as we waited for our flight back to beds – with mattresses.

It took a while to get over the shock of what we saw and to fit back into Australian society. Of all the three treks to the village, the first visit had the greatest impact on the team and myself. Within this adjustment time I put these thoughts down on paper.

Becoming part of the scene again requires learning afresh what the important issues of life are for those around me: knowing when to advise sympathetically, cluck admiringly or commiserate appropriately. At any other time, to offer such understanding intonations would have been easy. But now it is different because I am recovering from what I have seen in poverty-stricken areas in China. I visited a mountain village where the basics of water, food and money are scarce commodities. My senses are still jangling from the experience.

A bus ride and two plane flights transported me out of that valley of despair back to Australia and a people which deliberates long and hard over what to do with their disposable incomes and complain about our fluoridated, crystal-clear, drink-from-the-tap water in city areas! It is only with a great deal of grace that I muster any enthusiasm for a conversation about the latest video, computer software or other little importances which people hold so dear. The memories of children in dirty clothes, with ugly red marks on their necks as though re-inked fingers had drummed their tattoos, keeps floating in my brain. Is it a skin condition or something worse? Who knows?

It is hard to go back to a world where trifling matters hold sway over our most significant assets of time and money. The needs of people trapped by cycles of poverty in less developed countries rarely surface into our worlds. Seeing devastating poverty first-hand suddenly polarises the issues of life into the important and the trivial and one is never the same after the experience.

Ideally, I believe everyone should have such a shake-up in their lives, preferably before their system of values has been set in consumerism concrete. Instead of parents spending money on material luxuries for their children, perhaps the money could be saved to send them on an overseas trip. How different the world would be if, as a matter of course, every young person from a wealthy nation was sent on a visit to a Third World country? I realise the itinerary must be selective, to avoid the team becoming traumatised by sights they would be too young to cope with. Some 'tourist' and cultural activities should be included as well. How changed their worldview would be on their return. Their value system would never be the same again.

How different our foreign policy would be, especially relating to foreign aid, if those in power had had this exposure while young enough to be moved by the experience?

Time and money are precious commodities. They should not be wasted on the pursuit of 'little importances' but be used to pursue the big picture for the benefit of others, especially those unable to improve their own circumstances.

One young man who is using his time and profile for godly purposes is Andrew Bibby, better known as Lance Wilkinson on the long-running TV series *Neighbours*. As patron of Christian Blind Mission International (CBMI), he saw firsthand the results of cataract surgery on the lives of thousands of poor people in the Philippines. When he saw some of the work he is promoting, he remarked that during the previous year the patients had just been statistics on paper to him. But having seen them in person made the whole thing very real.

He was amazed: 'Everyone is still so happy. They have no idea that by western standards they have little [materially]. They get on with their life and they're thankful for everything they do have. It makes you re-evaluate everything you worry and care about in your life. The things we find important just pale into insignificance when you see these people with such drive and energy for life living in the midst of so little.'

Andrew was shocked by a comparison of salaries between Australia and the Philippines. The cataract operations are completed in only 15 minutes and for most patients are provided free of charge, or are the maximum princely sum of $27.

Simple and affordable by our standards, Andrew found he had to face the question of why more wasn't being done. 'One of the [Filipino] surgeons asked me how many days he'd have to work to earn $27 in Australia. I was stunned. It's like, Days? What? It would take maybe an hour-and-a-half for most people.' They think it must be a big thing for people to earn $27 because they've got such a lack of funding [from overseas] and they can't do as much work as they'd like to. I felt almost ashamed when I told him how little time it would take to earn $27.[2]

CBMI is a non-governmental organisation operating in developing countries with people who are blind, hearing-impaired and physically disabled. It works in co-operation with over six hundred mission agencies, local churches, developmental organisations and governments.

Andrew's reward for patronage came in seeing patients transformed once they could see. He said that while blind, the people just sat in their huts in almost trance-like states.

> It's as if nothing was going on in their mind; they were just bodies, beings. Once their sight was restored through an operation, they became alive. They were following things with their eyes and communicating with their children.[3]

The exposure trip lit a passion in Andrew to help people. He said he wants to use his fame on TV to grab attention and use it in a positive way to spread the word of God.

> *Let us more and more insist on raising funds of love, of kindness, of understanding, of peace. Money will come if we seek first the Kingdom of God – the rest will be given. (Mother Theresa)*

Christmas Children

Here is some mail that greeted me at Christmas – stark reminder of how much we really have and how much others need. (Adapted From World Vision of Australia advertising material)

NAME: Alli-Jayne
AGE: 8
LIVES: Melbourne, Australia

For an Aussie kid like Alli-Jayne, her greatest wish this Christmas is for a Mermaid Barbie.

Alli-Jayne already has Barbie dolls, but there always seems to be another one she 'needs'. The Barbies live on a special shelf, alongside three shelves of fairy-tales, picture-books and magazines.

Bounding up the hallway to Alli-Jayne's room comes the new puppy, Sam. She cost Alli-Jayne's Mum and Dad $250 (and $10 a week to feed), but to Alli-Jayne, Sam's priceless. And Alli-Jayne knows the value of money. There's $1.50 pocket money, $2 for the bank, $2.50 for Friday lunch order, $5 for gymnastics, and 50c for her school's child sponsorship…

Last week, when Alli-Jayne had a cough, the doctor was only two minutes away. And the chemist was open to 9 pm with the medicine prescribed. There wasn't even a day off school where Alli-Jayne dreams of learning to be a teacher – or a Spice Girl!

Spending money – $11.50 per week.

According to Dolly magazine, a 10 year-old girl in Australia has $13.88 spending power per week.

NAME: Ruma
AGE: 4
LIVES: Dhaka, Bangladesh

For a child like Ruma, her greatest wish is for something to stop the pain in her eyes.

Ruma is four years old, and she's going blind. The reason? Not some exotic disease with a long fancy name, but water. The contaminated water from the filthy pond that is the only water supply for Ruma, her family and the 120 other families who live in their slum.

The pond is used for drinking. And bathing. And cleaning dishes. And washing clothes…

The water burns Ruma's eyes and scars them. But that's not all. It gives Ruma and her friends dysentery, worms, diarrhoea – horrible sicknesses that ravage little bodies, and sap away all strength. There's no nearby doctor, no medicine her Mum and Dad can buy to make things get better.

As Ruma's sight fades to darkness, so does any hope of an education that will enable her to find a way out of the slum. Sponsorship - $7.15 per week (tax deductible). It costs so little to bring hope and happiness to a child in need.

Michael Griffiths of Overseas Missionary Fellowship wrote a missions book titled, *Give Up Your Small Ambitions*. The title was taken from the exhortation of Francis Xavier, the sixteenth-century Jesuit missionary to India, China, and Japan. Xavier is said to have longed to go back to Paris, shouting up and down the streets to tell the students to give up their small ambitions and come eastward to preach the gospel of Christ.[4]

'I want to show you the boy we've picked for our family!'

Meredith bobbed up and down at the table full of excitement that there was now a new member in her family. Her bright eyes studied the display of photographs of forlorn girls and boys staring at the camera, mixed emotions etched on their faces, elicited from painful experiences that should never have come into their short lives.

'There he is, that's ours,' she announced proudly pointing at a child. Below him was a blue spot. The spots under each photograph told the world that a local person or family had begun sponsoring the Indian boy or girl. Now the child had a Christian home in the orphanage and an education. The fifty children in the orphanage would hear about a Jesus who wept over the needs of this world and loved to death all his little ones.

Granted, this was a crude way to administer the sponsorship programme with numbers and spots and clinical data on each child. So cold and methodical. But the eagerness of the people flocking to the desk morning and evening over a few weeks to sign up and 'take a child home' with their hearts and wallets meant that their care and prayers would be constant and individual.

Just like Jesus loves us.

The people staffing the desk had a wonderful time giving out forms in all directions, answering questions that came by the dozen and even breaking up friendly 'disputes' when two people wanted to sponsor the same child. It was exciting to see all the children so quickly gain the badge of acceptance and hope in a prosperous future.

My name is Modula and I am nine years old. I come from a village called Nandipadu... My father died and my mother and two older brothers are daily wage labourers... I have polio... so my mother could not care for me properly. I am very happy to stay in the home along with the other children. Coming from a poor family I never thought of being educated. This children's home has made a difference in my life! I am being educated, I have food and above all, parental love in the home. I want to study hard and secure a good job so I can help support my family members. I love to play with the other children in any free time. I feel very much at home here and am very grateful and thankful to my sponsoring parents for supporting me and giving me this wonderful opportunity. I pray every day for my sponsor and praise God for giving me such wonderful people who care for me.

Modula Karuna lives in a Christian Outreach Ministries Home in the province of Andra Pradesh, India.

The Journey

Keith Greenwood from COM writes:

Who could ever have realised that God would use you and me to bring His blessing to so many people? God said to Abraham: 'And I will bless you, and you shall be a blessing to many nations' (Gen. 12:1–3). Is that not the purpose and call of all God's children? How can anyone trust Him if they have never heard of Him? How can they hear without someone to tell them? The answer to all the need in this world is the Gospel.

Keith was one of the blessed people who was born and brought up in a Christian home, went to a Christian school, a Christian church, married a Christian girl and had the privilege of seeing all three children become committed Christians. When he turned forty he thought he was right in the centre of what God wanted for his life, his church and his world. For some of us that is all we want and would be just as happy to go to be with the Lord then and there. He had little awareness that God had a global plan and he desires all his children to have a part in that too.

The Lord had a big task for Keith to handle – a task to help one of the densely populated countries in the world – India.

Keith went to India to take part in crusades in the early 1980s with International Outreach Ministries.

When I first stepped on Indian soil and saw the overwhelming need of that nation and the inability of me to do much about it, I felt hopeless. Nothing could have prepared me for the misery I saw in the city of Bombay. So many people in one place. So much poverty, so many sick and dying, whole families living on the sidewalk under a bit of plastic or rusty iron. Lepers, with half eaten fingers reaching out for food. All looking to me for help. I could not help them. I remember the desperation I felt not being able to help them. They needed food, medicines, clothes, housing, money. I had none of those to give them. Just to say 'God loves you' and then to leave them seemed hypocritical to me.

As he struggled with those emotions he prayed: 'God please help me to change my ticket tomorrow to go back home. What am I doing here?' (The last question sounds to me like a whisper from the enemy. He always fears what we can achieve when God is calling the shots in someone's life – and not him.)

Keith learnt that God uses these things to show us and prepare us for his purposes. 'God spoke to me ever so clearly: "Read Psalm 33:18." I had no idea what was in that psalm.'

> *The eyes of the Lord are upon those who fear Him,*
> *Upon those who trust in His unfailing love,*
> *To deliver them from death*
> *And keep them alive in famine. (NIV)*

This Psalm changed Keith's whole concept of why we are here as Christians on this earth, and to say the least, it changed his life and goals for the future when he realised:

1. What is the Lord looking for? A nation of people who acknowledge him and who trust in his unfailing love.
2. What would he do? Deliver them and keep them. He would provide for their needs.

That is a challenging and huge promise to all humanity. Keith knew that for thousands of years the nation of India looked to idols. The people did not know the true maker of heaven and earth, so God could not bless them. He remembered the words of Romans:

For 'whoever calls upon the name of the Lord shall be
saved.'
How then shall they call on Him in whom they have
not believed?
And how shall they believe in Him of whom they have
not heard?
And how shall they hear without a preacher?
And how shall they preach unless they are sent? (Rom.
10:13–15)

Instantly Keith saw it. God's plan for the world: for his church to fulfil that command to reach the world. When this gospel is preached to all nations then the end shall come, hastening the day of his coming.

Keith knew that this is not the task for a few missionaries alone but for the whole church. He paraphrased the Biblical command: 'Some go, some preach, others send, others pray, others make it possible. When the whole church sees this as God's heart and act on it, it will happen.'

He saw that God loved these people and that we had the answer for them. Five hundred million people in India alone have not yet heard the gospel, and we have the answer. Put into perspective:

1. Feed them? It's good but they will hunger again.
2. Clothe them? We must, but clothes wear out.
3. Bring the Gospel? They will have the answer to all of their needs now and forever.

God instantly gave Keith a passion that still drives him today. He courageously stayed in the country and preached God's promises. The 1981 team had the overwhelming privilege to see tens of thousands of people respond to the truth of God. That trip planted the vision from which COM was established. Keith is now the COM Director. Since that time he has tripped off to India more than forty times.

In 1984 four other people went to India to help Indian churches follow up those people who had responded at the crusade in Kakinada. Keith met Br M.S. Williams who interpreted while Keith preached the Gospel to rural village people. Thousands asked Jesus into their lives and many were healed. Blind and crippled people were miraculously restored and testified to the reality of God. Now there is a desperate need for Christian workers as the familiar verse states that the fields are ready for harvest but the labourers are few.

The son of a Hindu convert, Br Williams had just come into baptism of the Holy Spirit and was overflowing with zeal. He was at the time a teacher, working among college students in Kakinada when the team challenged him to leave his job and become an evangelist. It was a most daring step. He didn't know the Australians well and he knew that once he left his job, it would be unlikely that he would ever be able to return to it. But the zeal the Lord gave him to see people saved, persuaded him to accept his calling.

From that time onwards teams were sent from Australia to India regularly. A handful of Bible students also began to be trained. Soon after the first COM pastors were sent to their villages, they saw the pressing need to care and provide for orphaned and underprivileged children. Each pastor chose a number who were desperately needy. Australian sponsors were found to support these kids. He said the willingness for Australians to do this was great and in a few years sponsors were found for five hundred young ones.

> Together with faithful Indian Christians and thousands of Committed Christians in Australia we have established Christian Outreach Ministries. At this stage in year 2000 we have trained 1000 Indian workers who now work in 2000 villages and they have established 1500 churches. Australian Christians are now supporting destitute children in 24 children's homes, high schools and trade schools. We have medical ministries in 100 tribal villages with a doctor and 20 nurses ministering God's love to thousands.

As in 1981 when the story of India started for Keith and his family, fresh people and longer-term supporters of the work join the regular short-term trips to India. They work with pastors and every time God's plan repeats itself as thousands of Indians respond to the message they share and new churches are born. The ministry developed into a family affair with his wife Helen and daughter Christa taking care of two aspects of the ministry.

> Years ago deciding to be a missionary meant travelling to an unknown country and learning a language other than your own. The aim was to take the gospel to a

non-Christian country and win converts to Christianity – a vision missionaries hold today. However, there are many ways of being a missionary, including staying at home and supporting those who go off to far-flung places and live, sometimes in very difficult environments.

Helen visited India with her husband. 'When I saw the many needy children I wanted to go home and raise money to provide food and shelter for them.'

It was some years before her role as a missionary began. After her children had grown up, Helen opened an Opportunity Shop and with the help of other ladies saw this 'opportunity' blossom into a full time ministry. Their commitment and love have made a difference in the lives of hundreds of Indian orphans. For almost ten years, the annual proceeds of approximately $40,000 have been used to establish children's homes, providing for the children until support comes from the foster care scheme, businesses and churches. There are now twenty-four homes, and besides financial provision, each year a container of clothes is shipped to India. For Helen and her dedicated team of ladies, their joy is in knowing that many children have benefited from this ministry.[5]

Christa writes:

In 1989 I felt God telling me to go to India on a mission trip to see for myself what my Dad was always talking about. I was so moved I went back again the following year. God had planted a seed in my heart. I'd always wanted my life to count for some thing and I realised I could make a difference in India. However God still had some work to do in my life, so for a time this call was put on hold. In August 1998 I was personally challenged by a good friend to really find out what God would have me do in the new year. With fear and trepidation I sought God and He opened up a number of options… I made the decision to work part time so that I could give God the rest. Now I am working for COM two days a week, and I know this is just the beginning. I feel honoured to be a part of COM, but also awed by the task ahead. I thank God for this amazing opportunity.[6]

Keith simply states:

All God requires is willing hearts to work through. The last years have proven that much can be done if many people together feel God's heart and start to put this in action. We are confident that this will continue to happen. This gives us great satisfaction and confidence in an exciting future.[7]

Therefore we make it our aim, whether present or absent, to be well pleasing to Him. For we must all appear before the Judgement seat of Christ, that each one may receive the things done in the body, according to what he has done, whether good or bad. Knowing, therefore, the terror of the Lord, we persuade men; but we are well known to God, and I also trust are well known in your consciences. (2 Cor. 5:9)

---

[1] Collins Paperback Encyclopedia, HarperCollins Glasgow 1998
[2] Maroun, pp. 20–21

[3] Maroun, p. 20
[4] Griffiths, quoted in Borthwick, p. 155
[5] 'Opportunity', *COM Newsletter*, May 2000
[6] Greenwood, C., *COM Newsletter*, April 1999
[7] Account is a combination of Keith Greenwood's own testimony and stories from *COM Newsletter*, vol. 3, no. 1 April 1999

6

Belt up

'George, put your seatbelt on please,' I said tapping him on the shoulder. 'Just in case we have an accident.'

My slight though deliberate tone of bossiness worked. Chatter, chatter in Chinese by George resulted in the driver obediently doing likewise. I relaxed. I had no reason to relax in one sense. They had the seatbelts, there were none fitted in the back seat where I was.

'Well, Lord you will have to watch over us all, then,' I prayed.

We set out on a twelve-hour journey to Guangzhou. By Australian standards it wasn't long – 560 kilometres. But the highway instead of skirting towns as many Australian highways do, linked up each town and village along the way. Needless to say, travelling mercies were needed to safely steer us through continuous rivers of local and long-distance traffic of all descriptions. Trucks, small and agile and large and lumbering, motorbikes, bicycles, horse-drawn carts, vans with regis-

tration numbers emblazoned in paint on their
backs, and a variety of cars jostled for space on the
road. At least the highway was concrete and not
dirt. The purpose of our journey was to pick up my
Australian friend who had come to also teach with
me at my college. After collecting her from
Guangzhou airport, there was another twelve-hour
journey before us in reverse, before we arrived back
'home'.

Putting on a seatbelt is such an automatic action
in Australia: usually only small children need to be
reminded. Belt-wearing is compulsory in Australia
but car safety is lightly regarded in China. That is
surprising given the vast volume of traffic: from
bicycles to semi-trailers cramming Chinese roads
and highways. How would the police enforce it
properly with such a vast population?

Someone who had a 'reverence for life' and
believed in the 'eternity of life' was Dr Peter King,
who saved many lives and injuries through his pioneer work to introduce seatbelt legislation. A
devout Christian, Dr King (1939–98) once thought
that he might become a medical missionary.
However, God had a plan for Peter to make a contribution to humanity on a scale not restricted to
one locality such as his own State of Victoria,
Australia but to impact many nations.

As a young man he loved fast cars and planes.
He delighted in driving his red Ferrari around the
Victorian country town of Shepparton where he

was practising medicine. His passion for speed led him to become a track medical officer at Sandown and Calder Raceways in Melbourne.

In 1966 he noticed that the racing drivers who wore seatbelts regularly emerged from severe crashes unscathed. He asked a motorsport engineer to fit similar belts to those used in racing cars to his family car and took his findings to the Royal Australasian College of Surgeons (RACS). For many years he was a member of RACS.

He spoke at the seminar 'The Management of Road Traffic Casualties' conducted by RACS in October 1969.

Most of the morbidity and some of the mortal injuries can be prevented by the correct use of suitable seat belts. Legislation must be made to provide the compulsory provision of lap-sash belts in all motor vehicles. As doctors, we must provide a stimulus to the intensive education of the people on this matter and provide information of the injuries caused by the wrongly applied seat belt or by the use of an inadequate type of seat belt (e.g. lap type). Moreover, the people should be made aware of the value of well-designed head rests in the prevention of injuries to the neck. I hasten to add that after four years attendance at motor race circuits I have seen thirty-six significant crashes in touring car events, yet have only given treatment for bruises. One vehicle, after crashing at 120 mph disintegrated with the exception of the tubular steel cage and attached harness in which the driver was perfectly well secured – he sustained a fractured finger. It is compulsory in motor racing for drivers to wear full racing restraining harness and helmet. I am sure that the compulsory use of seat belts will save lives, save hospital beds and save the nation a great deal of money.[1]

The story from the time of Peter King's recommendation until the adoption of the legislation reads like a case study for a PR textbook: the effect of his words on the hearts of hearers set in train a series of remarkable events which culminated in seatbelt legislation. The measure was recommended to the Victorian Government who passed the first such legislation in the world. Eventually many other countries followed suit with their own compulsory enforcement.

The College (RACS) was not the first to propose compulsory seatbelts but it was the tenacity of their campaign that won through in the end. The Road Trauma Committee tabled the following events in a report to the College Council.

The RACS Road Trauma Committee 1970-75 gave to the Legislative Assembly several recommendations such as a public education programme. Little happened. So they sought an interview from *The Age* newspaper. The resulting article appeared on 17 June 1970 outlining the seriousness of the situation and concern of surgeons. In a tragic irony 17 people were killed on Victorian roads that weekend.

Mr Don Gibb, Promotions Consultant read the article and offered his services in a voluntary capacity to the Road Trauma Committee to promote belt-wearing and public awareness about drink driving.

The Committee accepted his services and launched a six-month publicity campaign in Melbourne, Adelaide and Sydney. The media took up the cause emphasising the horrendous injuries incurred from smashes; *The Daily Telegraph*, Sydney, the *Australian Women's Weekly*, and *The Sun*, Melbourne, to name a few. The latter wrote: 'Surgeons were sick and tired of seeing road accident victims jellied up, their faces smashed and spines paralysed.'[2]

Hector Crawford, the television producer agreed to ensure that his 'police' in films wore seatbelts. Soon afterwards the Victorian Police Force announced publicly that all staff were to wear belts – with no exceptions. (Usually the government makes the first move and the public second.)

In November 1970 RACS received another win. The Federal Government acknowledged how serious the problem was by establishing an Expert Group to advise the minister in charge of National Road Safety. RACS President Mr P.J. Kenny was appointed to this group.

Success was achieved when Sir Arthur Rylah, Chief Secretary and Deputy Premier of Victoria, introduced the mandatory wearing of seatbelt legislation on 22 December 1970. Despite some doubts from other politicians (why, one asks?) the community readily accepted the legislation. By 1973 all states had adopted the laws.

Other countries began to take notice and accept the life-saving facts. In a letter to the British Medical Journal on Safer Motoring the noted accident surgeon, William Gissane, concluded: 'Perhaps, after all, the Australian legislators were right in introducing compulsory seat belt wear even at this stage of belt design development.'[3]

Statistical results from hospital records confirmed that opinion. At the 45th General Scientific Meeting of the RACS in Hobart in 1972, Fellows were presented with facts relating to seatbelts. Dr J.E.K. Galbraith, from the Austin Hospital in Melbourne stated that there were substantial reductions in eye injuries from car accidents. The RACS Pattern of Injury Survey showed the higher mortality amongst those who did not wear belts and lower probability of severe injury to the body for those wearing them.

There were further initiatives by the RACS. A paediatric surgeons sub-committee of the RACS Road Trauma Committee later took on the task of finding a suitable harness for children travelling in cars.

All his professional life Peter King was keen to advance and improve medical services to the community. His life showed a compassion and energetic involvement in medicine. But he had to overcome problems to get his qualifications. To get into medicine at Melbourne University, he had to overcome dyslexia.

He later served as registrar in plastic and reconstructive surgery at the Preston & Northcote Community Hospital before moving to the Austin Hospital in Melbourne. Six years after graduation he was awarded a fellowship in the RACS. He trained as a vascular surgeon during his post-graduate studies in London, Minnesota, Christchurch and several Australian capitals, then taught at several medical schools.

Rather than set up practice in Melbourne, he chose to go to the country. He married Denise Polan in 1964 and six years later became the medical superintendent of the Goulburn Valley Base Hospital, Shepparton. Peter came close to the reality of car smashes through the tragic death of a fellow surgeon. This left Peter as the only surgeon in the city. But through Peter's enthusiasm and endeavours to attract medical staff, in 1999 20 surgeons looked after the Goulburn-Murray region.

In part fulfilling his desire to become a medical missionary to a developing country, he accepted the call by RACS to go to Port Moresby for six months during the mid-1980s. As a professor he taught surgery and established the Chair of Surgery at the University of Papua New Guinea as well as travelling to outlying centres. The link formed by that relationship has continued to this day in the regular visits of PNG surgeons to RACS and the Provincial Surgeons' Association. Denise King, his wife recalls that some of them when they met Peter in Australia would say: 'Hi Professor, how you going?' It was a busy time for him in PNG and Peter returned to Australia just the day before his daughter was married.

Peter also responded to another RACS request for a surgeon to go to the Butterworth Air Force Base in Malaysia. He went over for a second term, again of three months duration in 1988. While he was there he met many people on the Base and was deeply grieved when one of his friends died in a plane crash.

Peter was very good at working in with other people, especially in extensive committee work, so his achievements should always be seen within the context of the activities of other committee members. Drs Peter MacNeil and Ian Gunn commented in their obituary about Peter: 'Both as a leader and a country colleague the personal touches he brought to what he did and the positions he held will be warmly remembered. Who will ever forget his sense of humour and the way he could bring to life a rather dull meeting with his humorous comments and by telling one or two outrageous jokes.'

Despite a busy life, his many other interests included training paramedics in the Goulburn Valley ambulance service, accident trauma, malignant melanoma and researching vascular disease.

He wanted to improve medical services in country areas to bring them on par with metropolitan services. Since the early 1970s he was addressing the conditions and disadvantages for surgeons residing in the country. Five years before his death, he and a team of people including Dr Ian Gunn in Shepparton, undertook a national survey of rural surgical services and practices. His findings that rural areas were poorly served brought him nationwide recognition. He proposed to the RACS that a new training programme especially developed for surgery in rural areas be established.

He was a member of the RACS Council for a number of years and in 1993 Peter became Chairman of the Divisional Group of Rural Surgery as well as being honoured by life membership to that Group. A crowning success of his efforts as Chairman was the Rural Surgical Training Programme for which the Federal Government provided long-term funding. The Federal Minister of Health hailed the programme as the best Rural Specialist Training Programme he had seen. There were 30 surgical trainees in the year 2000 programme.

He formed a board of graduate studies in the Goulburn Valley Hospital and was a driving force behind the building of the Shepparton Private Hospital.

Dr Gordon Trinca from RACS had known Peter for over thirty years since his days at Preston. He said that Peter had been a strong supporter of college initiatives directed at reducing road trauma including occupant restraint legislation, drink driving countermeasures, compulsory helmet wearing for pedal cyclists and later the development of the optimum trauma care services. After his death in 1998, the College of Surgeons Council endowed the Peter King Perpetual Scholarship for the advancement of rural surgery.

The King children remember him as one who always made time for important family events like organising their birthday parties. He taught at the Sunday School of their church as well as gave Christian education in primary schools for about ten years. He conducted a forum each Wednesday lunchtime at Scots Church, Shepparton. The event took many forms: music, talks or debates on current issues. Robert Brown commented in *The Age*:

> Intelligent and practical faith was the centre-point of
> Peter King's life. He believed not simply in life after
> death, but in eternal life… He accepted the promise of

peace of mind through forgiveness, a growing understanding of what it meant to love, and power to live
confidently and with integrity.

Colin Smith, the RACS archivist commented:

Looking over his activities, I see a rather inspiring
person. A person with a finger in quite a lot of pies,
who was always thinking of ways to improve the general decency of life – whether it was to reduce the
number of dead people being dragged out of wrecked
cars; [or] to get more good surgeons into country
areas.

Two colleagues Drs Peter MacNeil and Ian Gunn
gave this tribute:

Rural surgery lost a forceful advocate with the sad
death of Peter King... Like many outstanding figures
in the surgical profession and in the ranks of country
surgeons, Peter will be seen as a unique figure. His
achievements are indeed a fitting monument by which
we will remember him... Peter's achievements were
possible because of the constant support provided by
Denise, Gary, Janine and Kathryn. The inner strength
of the King family was very evident during Peter's last
brave battle with cancer.

His wife Denise, their three children and four
grandchildren survive him. But in a sense also sur-
viving him are all those people who emerged, like
the racing car drivers, from horrific accidents with
their lives – because they wore seatbelts.

I am intrigued by this next story which leads into the next chapter 'When there is a Job to be Done'. This woman's persistence to bring her vision to fruition, despite her own grief, is an example to me. Ruth Senter tells the story;

I have often wondered exactly what Jesus meant when he said, 'No one who puts his hand to the plow and looks back is fit for service in the Kingdom of God' (Luke 9:62). Recently, I got a glimpse of what I think he meant.

I read the story on the wall of a Foreigner's Clinic in Seoul, South Korea. I'd come to see the American doctor for a routine inoculation. The story on the wall was about his mother, who along with her husband had been a missionary to Korea for many years.

One day, the woman's husband was involved in an automobile accident. At this time in Seoul, there were no emergency vehicles to call. The only transport to the hospital was by taxi. The missionary, still in the prime of life, died in the taxi on his way to the hospital.

Many wives, less stout-hearted, would have packed their bags and headed for home. Or at least, gotten angry. [Yes, I would have done that. No more heroic missionary service or aspiring to greatness in the kingdom for me!] But not this missionary wife. She immediately began raising funds to buy emergency vehicles for the city of Seoul. She gathered enough money from friends and acquaintances, many of them in the United States, to purchase and equip the city's first ambulance. Then she persuaded medical emergency specialists from her home country to come to Korea and donate their time to lead the first-ever training sessions for Korean paramedics.

Today, ambulances are a common sight in South Korea. People continue to equip them with the latest in modern technology and personnel training. Now, whenever I see a green and white emergency vehicle, I think: It all began with one brave missionary wife, who, when she 'put her hand to the plow' did not look back, even in the face of great personal loss.

May God give us more of her kind.[4]

---

[1] King, p. 29
[2] *The Sun*, 28 July 1970, quoted by Hughes, p. 6
[3] Hughes, p. 8
[4] Senter, 108

7

When there is a Job to be Done

*Thousands of Australians lie buried in the countries of
the eastern Mediterranean, from Tobruk in Libya
around the coast to Egypt and modern Israel, through
Jordan, Lebanon and Syria to Turkey and Greece,
including Crete.*[1]

One of the characteristics of the Australian persona
is our 'larrikinism', defined as 'a person who acts
with apparent disregard for social or political con-
ventions'. Larrikinism can drift into troublemaking.
But it is part of our national identity and has played
a role in making our nation develop into what it is
today. I have included war efforts in this chronicle
of humanitarians, not to glorify war by any means,
nor to impute godliness into the men who fought in
the Middle East. But larrikinism springs from lateral thinking as demonstrated by the Charge at
Beersheba by the Australian Light Horse. They
thought out a solution which was against military
paradigms and succeeded where thousands others
had failed throughout the centuries.

Why is this event important today? As mentioned in 'Feeling with Mind and Soul', God is call-

ing people who are also lateral thinkers to take part in his great commission to reach the nations. He is opening up varieties of ways to touch the unreached – all he needs are risk-takers and supporters behind them. He is the one who brings success.

The Australian Light Horse were part of the Egyptian Expeditionary Force (EEF) as it entered Sinai in August 1916 and began the campaign pushing the Turks back from the canal at Romani on the coast. Many of the Light-horsemen were survivors of Gallipoli, now reunited with their horses.

Some of the horses for the Australian Light Horse used in World War One battles were broken-in wild brumby stock, from harsh areas such as desert regions and the Kimberley Ranges in Western Australia. So they were aptly suited to the demands of war.[2]

More than thirty thousand Australian men fought in the Australian Light Horse during the First World War. By the end of the War, the number of enlisted men was 416,809. Over half the eligible white male population of Australia enlisted, 80 per cent of these served overseas, mostly in France.

By proportion of population New Zealand then Australia suffered the largest number of casualties in the War. It was an enormous effort because our population at the time was only four million. We were not fighting on our own soil.

The German and Turkish forces were controlling the whole of the Middle East, from Suez to Palestine and Syria. The British Generals Phillip Chetwode and from June 1917, Edmund 'Bull' Allenby headed the campaign in those countries. Harry Chauvel (who became Sir Harry Chauvel in January 1917) commanded the three divisions of the Desert Mounted Corps comprising all of the mounted soldiers: Australian, New Zealand, British and Indian, horses and camels. Lawrence of Arabia led the Arab Army as they fought from the desert of the Hejaz in Arabia, to the Jordan River towards Damascus and Aleppo. Chauvel's men were part of the successful battles in this campaign, beginning with Romani in August 1916, Gaza in March and April 1917, the charge at Beersheba in October, the Jordan River at Es Salt and Amman (City of the Ammonites) in April 1918 and Megiddo in September. But the climax came with the taking of Damascus on 1 October 1918.

> It was Chauvel's strategic and tactical sense added to the bravery and elan of the Light-horsemen that won these battles and created new legends in these most legendary lands. Chauvel was, with Sir John Monash, one of the two great Australian commanders of large forces in World War I, which makes him one of the greater generals of history. In this part of the world that is the highest praise, because these battlefields have tested the best light cavalry for 5000 years.[3]

Beersheba (modern day Be'er Sheva) is mentioned in a catchphrase in the Bible; 'From Dan to Beersheba' referring to 'from north to south of the country' inferring the entire nation or population. During biblical times the city marked the southern

boundary of Israel. Abraham swore an oath with
Abimelech and dug a well there (Gen. 21:22–34).
Situated on the semi-arid edge of the Negev Desert,
it served as Beersheba's own defence. The wells
there have been of paramount significance for thousands of years.

Beersheba had to be taken or the sixty thousand
British troops and the Australian troops and horses
would perish from lack of water. After 12 hours of
attack, the British were no nearer to taking the walls
of Beersheba. So they had as we say: 'Two chances,
slim and Buckley's.' The horses had not drunk for
two days.

Grant, an Australian commander, proposed a
mounted charge on the east wall.

The horsemen had experienced the tragic effects
of bungling at Gallipoli in 1915. But at Beersheba
the eight hundred of them were on their Australian
horses and under Australian authority so 'the Light
Horse joyfully, it seems, defied military wisdom,
and with swords in hand and Adam Lindsay
Gordon (Australian poet) on their lips, stormed the
Turkish defences.'[4]

The assault took only 30 minutes and accomplished what a one thousand years of Crusaders
and other insurgents had failed to do.

The official historian of the Palestine and Syria
campaign, Harry Gullett, wrote:

> At Beersheba the usual tactics of the Anzacs, though
> exercised to the full, were found inadequate to over-
> come the opposition; and the Light Horsemen, appear-
> ing in a new role, threw caution and cunning to the

winds and snatched victory at the last moment in a
blind, wild, headlong gallop. The day was on the
wane, it was now neck or nothing. There was a brief
but tense discussion, in which Fitzgerald and Grant
pleaded for the honour of the galloping attack which
was clearly in Chauvel's mind. Fitzgerald's (British)
yeomanry had their swords and were close behind
Chauvel's headquarters. Grant's Australians had only
their rifles and bayonets, but they were nearer
Beersheba. After a moment's thought, Chauvel gave
the lead to the Light Horsemen. 'Put Grant straight at
it,' was his terse command.[5]

(I am pleased accuracy prevailed in the Australian
film of this military triumph *Charge of the Light
Horse* and that famous command was quoted by
'Chauvel'.)

Under conventional military practice the Light
Horse did not go into battle with cavalry swords,
but carried rifles with bayonets instead. They
would ride to the battleground, dismount, take
cover and then fight the enemy. There are rules to
these practices, remember.

To the surprise of the startled Turks, these
Aussies instead, jumped straight over lines upon
lines of entrenched Turkish infantry, entrenched
artillery and machine guns, dodging most of the
fire. Once behind the entrenched enemy, some
troops charged the wall and seized the vital wells,
while others dismounted and captured the Turkish
Division.[6]

Unlike Gallipoli where 8709 men died largely
through military incompetence, this charge only

cost 31 lives and 32 were wounded out of eight hundred horsemen.

The success of the mounted charge of Beersheba unlocked the Turkish defensive position in Southern Palestine and set in motion a chain reaction of victories. In its third battle, Gaza was captured in November and Jerusalem on 9 December 1917. Amman was taken on 26 September 1918 by part of the Australian 5th Light Horse and New Zealand's Canterburys. Turkish resistance collapsed when they saw the Queenslanders of the 7th Light Horse.

Ironically, one year less one day after the charge, on 30 October 1918, the Turks sued for an armistice – the war in this theatre was finished.

> The Australian charge at Beersheba was the last successful cavalry charge in warfare, and Chauvel's very Australian order, 'Put Grant straight at it' a fitting culmination of the spirit of cavalry action.[7]

Lawrence of Arabia complimented the Light Horse in his Seven Pillars of Wisdom by saying that they regarded war as a type of 'point to point' race.

At the thanksgiving service after victory the Rev Maitland Woods rather poetically commented: 'I would describe the light-horseman as a man who, while denying he is a Christian, practises all the Christian virtues.'[8]

In December 1917 women of Jerusalem strewed palm leaves in front of the victorious Aussies as they entered the city. Others wept as the monks sang *Kyrie Eleison, Christ Eleison* at midnight Mass to celebrate the birth of Christ.

The fact that the soldiers were riding through lands rich in vast history and religious devotion and conflict was not lost on them. Gullett wrote of their entry into Jerusalem:

> They rode with the strong purpose of old soldiers, but still with the sharp expectancy of happy travellers venturing into a famous land touched with mystery and hallowed by religion, history and tradition, all more or less familiar to them since their childhood... The men of the 2nd Light Horse Brigade at Jerusalem and the Camel Brigade at Bethlehem were for the first time in the Holy Places... they explored the cities with the zest of pilgrims... The curiosity of the men was boundless; and the diligent reading of the Old and New Testaments, combined with a true reverence, strangely broken by sceptical challenges and even lapses into daring, good-humoured blasphemy, imposed a heavy strain on the physical endurance [and] the biblical knowledge of the regimental padres. From daylight to dark these good men walked the many ways of Christ at the head of successive parties of troopers, who enjoyed nothing so much as 'to take a fall' out of their guides. Full of significant suggestion was this spectacle of young Australian Light Horsemen, led by churchmen in military dress and emu feathers, heavy boots, and clinking spurs, pro-ceeding along the Via Dolorosa or gathered round the traditional Stations of the Cross.[9]

An example of larrikinism at Beersheba can be seen in the life of Tibby Cotter. He was a well-known Sydney cricketer, a fast bowler with a slinging action similar to modern day Jeff Thomson. He was known for breaking stumps and bails. Before Beersheba he showed his prowess by hitting the stumps 18 out of 24 times with mud balls. He said to his mate: 'That's my last bowl, Blue; something is going to happen.'

As part of the 12th Light Horse, Private Cotter was distinguished at the second Gaza battle. People saw in him a fearless soldier. His larrikin spirit took him to Beersheba; he should have been at head-quarters on guard duty instead.

> His friend Blue recounted: 'Tibby was a great scrounger, liable to turn up in the middle of the desert with a bottle of champagne'. On the morning of the charge he said to Blue: 'I've skittled a Turk in one hit; and what do you think he had on him? Here it is – a yard of ling'. He promised the men a fish supper. Tibby, a mounted stretcher-bearer, was shot by a machine gun while riding next to Blue. After the charge Blue found him still alive.
>
> 'Blue,' said Tibby, 'you can have the fish supper on your own.' He died soon after.[10]

Weary Dunlop

Dedication in the War Diaries of Weary Dunlop:

> To those prisoners-of-war of several nations whose courage and fortitude uplifted me during dark days. The many dead are hallowed in my memory and the friendship of those living is one of life's precious

gifts. I pray that 'they shall hunger no more, neither thirst any more; neither shall the sun light on them nor any heat.' (The Revelation of St. John the Divine vii:16)

I could write volumes about the sacrificial work of Edward E. 'Weary' Dunlop as a surgeon in the prisoner-of-war camps in Java and the Burma-Thailand Railway during World War Two. He treated desperately ill men, emaciated by starvation, excessive physical labour and brutality by the Japanese with the most primitive, makeshift medical instruments. The following quote gives an idea of the difficulties and heartaches of fighting a war on foreign soil.

Weary wrote in his diary dated 22 July 1943:

Total in camp 367; hospital 337. Today was another severe reverse from the point of view of cholera deaths (6), including Jimmy Findlay, a quiet, semi-bald, sandy-haired little Salvationist... He had no strength to speak of and was old for this terrible grind out here, but quietly and heroically stuck it cheerfully for months, only to be done in by this cholera in the end, and finally so defeated as to beg to be 'finished off'. No more struggling out to work on lame and bleeding feet without boots. Sgt. Cowan, who died today, was typical of the well-off Australian landowner who came away in the ranks. I was looking at a picture of his wife and children today and the incongruity of things struck me – that men with comparative peace, comfort and security at home should be obliged to go to war and to suffer hunger, hardships and privation along a grim road leading to such a miserable death in a little quagmire in the jungle.[11]

He gave due credit to men around him who also gave so much for the sake of others. He mentioned a devoted medical staff member, S/Sgt Alan Gibson, who himself was suffering badly with dysentery, shivering with malaria and diminished to 'a near-naked skeleton'. But despite this he pulled his own blanket over a naked man, racked with cholera. The blanket was 'the last shred of comfort in the world... Only those ill, emaciated and thin, who slept... in all weathers, could comprehend his depth of sacrifice.'[12]

Weary saw the larrikin spirit in some of the men. Back in Australia Donald Stuart was a miner, bushman, horseman, outback drover, writer and continued to be a larrikin, in the death camps of Burma. Weary described him: 'Naked, except for bits and pieces strung round him like bizarre decorations, half a hat on his straw hair, he'd stalk past Japanese officers, refusing to salute. He was forever getting bashed up because of this. Yet every time he passed me his arm flashed up in the snappiest salute you ever saw.'[13] Stuart understood and respected where true authority lay.

But for Dunlop the story does not end with the end of the war. Not surprisingly, he nurtured during imprisonment a burning hatred of the Japanese but an incident became a turning point in his attitudes, actions and future endeavours in Australia and Asian countries after the war. He tells the story:

In the closing phases of the war, I was confronted with a train-load of Japanese casualties of the Burma campaign, in wretched condition, on a chaotic, over-crowded and often interrupted journey via the Burma-Thailand Railway. I paused before a man whose wretchedness equalled the plight of many of my own men – one leg had been hacked off at the mid-thigh and the bony stump projected through gangrenous flesh; his eyes were sunken pools of pain in a haggard, toxic face. With indomitable spirit he had hopped through hundreds of suffering miles without care. Some bombs fell and soldiers desperately fought for a place on the moving train. I moved to help him when he was trampled under in the rush, but his hand was limp and dead and the tortured face at peace. The memory dwelt with me as a lingering nightmare and I was deeply conscious of the Buddhist belief that all men are equal in the face of suffering and death. This conviction has grown during long years of preoccupation with Australian-Asian relationships generally and with several visits to Japan itself. On one of these, I was honoured to be able to escort a dying Japanese diplomat, who was my patient, on an eventful journey back to Japan and the comfort of his loved ones. Surely some increased understanding should emerge from a tragic conflict in which when all is said and done, Japanese losses vastly exceeded our own.[14]

During the years subsequent to the war until his death in 1993, Weary embraced many involvements with Asian nations, the Colombo Plan work in Thailand, Sri Lanka and India, civilian surgical work in South Vietnam and post-graduate medical exchanges with most of the Asian-Pacific countries. This medical work which helped in the development of these countries, replaced the hatred that he had felt during his war experiences. Instead he came to see that all races carry some special mark of God's tenderness, some unique contribution to humanity.

To put this wisdom into practice, Weary established The Sir Edward Weary Dunlop Asia Awards (trust of The University of Melbourne and administered by Asialink).

The pamphlet about the awards stated:

> Dunlop Asia Awards recognise unique Australians exemplifying Weary Dunlop's spirit of humanitarian service and commitment to Asia-Australia relations. Its three programs collectively seek to ensure that Weary's life and example remain a source of inspiration to all Australians.

Dunlop Asia Fellowships provide opportunities for young Australians to pursue study or work projects of a charitable nature within Fellowship-holders' host countries. Mr John Dore PhD candidate from The Australian National University, received the most recent award.

The Dunlop Asia Medal is awarded annually to a person who has shown commitment to enhancing the quality of life within the region and contributing to improve Australia-Asia relations. Mr Stephen Fitzgerald, the Chairman of the Australian Asia Institute, received the most recent award.

The Dunlop Asialink Lecture features an eminent orator on Australia-Asia relations offering challenging views to community leaders, and provides an annual occasion to remember Sir Edward's life and work. Past speakers have included the Australian Prime Minister the Rt Hon John Howard, United Nations High Commissioner for Refugees, HE Mrs Sadako Ogata and Cambodian Minister for International Co-operation, HE Ung Huot.[15] The most recent speaker was Lieutenant General John Sanderson, former Chief of the Australian Army and Chairman of the Consilium Group and PAXIQUEST Consulting on Australia's Millennial Shift – *A New Role in Asia?*

East Timor: Not Paradise Lost?

The sickening violence in East Timor, our government's response to this outrage, and the refugee camp in Darwin each enforce the fact that only the slender Timor Sea separates us from our northern neighbour. Australia's connection with East Timor goes back many decades prior to its seizure from Portugal by Indonesia in 1975. To be concerned with this vulnerable island is the only right humanitarian option for a friendly and close neighbour like Australia. Conversely some Indonesians regard our involvement as an unfriendly act: that we should mind our own business.

When the international peacekeeping force entered East Timor (1999)… the capital, Dili, was still burning

and its destruction almost complete. Dili's residents –
those who had escaped the violence – had fled for
their lives into the surrounding hills and further afield.
They were shocked, hungry and too terrified to move.
Cacilda Fernandez, a former midwife, says she has no
idea what the future holds for her and her children, 5-
year old Jose Vasilio, 3-year old Maria and eighteen-
month old, Jose Ernesto Junior. All she can do now is
live 'day by day'. Her husband, an outspoken
Economics and English teacher, was last seen by
Cacilda when he left for work on August 22. In early
September, she was told by an eyewitness that both
her husband and her brother-in-law had been mur-
dered. Her life and that of her children's, was also in
danger. So Cacilda fled with her family from Dili, ending up in a military camp that she says was more like
a concentration camp – with little food, no sanitation
and severely over-crowded. They were lucky to survive – many didn't. Now, with three children to raise
on her own, she is worried about her future, especially how she will feed them. She talks of returning to
work, but has no one to care for her children. For the
time being, she can only hope that things will get better.[16]

I visited Timor in the days when Australians called
it Portuguese rather than East Timor. Prior to 1975,
Portuguese not Indonesian soldiers roamed the
streets and bumped along rutted roads in army
trucks.

Despite this constant military presence, Timor
for me, as a high school kid, was a magical place
holding all the superlatives of 'Paradise': tall, wav-

ing coconuts, warm water (I think without sea wasps) lapping golden beaches. My first view of Timor as we flew over the mountains made geography lessons come graphically to life. I distinctly remember thinking how exactly the patchwork of the mountains, clouds, rivers and paddy fields matched the textbook descriptions of Asia. It was a country of coffee plantations in the highlands, industrious farmers on the lowlands, monkeys in jungles (and on the plate!), nimble-footed goats by the thousands, flooded rivers and over-sized wicker armchairs arranged on hotel balconies.

I went on a school trip organised by Darwin High School. Going to Timor then was as commonplace to a Darwinite as going down south – but a much shorter distance. Darwin to Dili as the crow flies is only a little over seven hundred kilometres. The short flight by TAA was not the only lesson about the close proximity of Timor to Australia. After a few days sight-seeing around Dili and Bacau, we drove to Tutuala on the northern tip of the island. The hotel was perched on a high cliff overlooking the Banda Sea. To one side of the cliff was verdant jungle with palm trees which seemed like saplings from such a height. While waiting for dinner one night, my classmates and I voiced our pangs of homesickness.

'I wanna eat a meat pie,' one said. I opted for an imaginary chocolate milkshake. The hotel staff solved our homesickness by turning on the radio. Loud and clear we heard a Radio Australia announcer. The distance between Darwin and Timor narrowed instantly for me since my father was at that time the supervising technician of the Radio Australia transmitters at Cox Peninsula, Darwin.

The population comprising mainly Timorese, Chinese and Portuguese co-existed in scattered townships. My teenage mind didn't take in the power plays between each of these ethnic groups. Nor could I have foreseen the intrusion of the Indonesians onto centre stage from 1975 to today with their genocide and scorched-earth policy.

The TV pictures of Timorese people praying and the emphatic remarks by Bishop Belo upon his arrival in Darwin reminded me of the Catholic service our group attended one night in Dili. The interior of the church was dark save for the flicker of candles held by each quiet worshipper. Though the priest conducted the Mass in Portuguese and the only word I could translate was 'Christ', I sensed the congregation's sincere devotion to God and his reassuring presence amongst us.

The male/female imbalance in the population intrigued me. Someone told us that there were about six men to every woman. If correct, this was probably due to the huge number of single Portuguese soldiers in the country. Passers-by stared at us wherever we went and sometimes it seemed as though whole streets stopped their business to look in our direction. Such attention continued inside the hotel. The staff hired a dance band for a couple of nights because our largely female group was staying there – much to the pleasure of the local male population. I was pleased that the first on the floor were a Portuguese soldier and myself!

Louis was a soldier on national service who had escaped from his army post in the mountains to spend some R & R in Dili. Fed up with the tropics, male company and loneliness, he desperately wanted to go back to his familiar Portugal and trade his army uniform for a business suit by working in his father's clothing factory. (But he was great on the dance floor.)

At the end of the holiday came the last reminder of Darwin's close proximity to Timor. When I spoke glowingly of Louis and the romantic time I had in Dili, my mother was characteristically horrified. Her 'pregnant-with-meaning' sighs said it all. Then came the lecture.

'You are not going to write to him. What if he comes to Darwin to see you? Remember Darwin is only a short distance from Timor!'

His letters landed in the rubbish bin but the more recent images on the TV screen elicit memories of Dili, Bacau and Tutuala and all the other towns we saw in between – and the people. I look back on these vivid memories of people and places, not with sentimental eyes but with a prayer for the Timorese to rebuild their communities, regenerate their environment and agriculture, develop self-government and freely worship.

Before the massacres, looting and burning and before the brave desire for self-determination, East Timor produced coffee, coconuts, maize and rice. Let's pray that it won't be long before the islanders

can fully concentrate on their livelihoods and community affairs and put behind them memories of
running for their lives.

> *War is not a polite recreation, but the vilest thing in*
> *life and we ought to understand that and not play at*
> *war. We ought to accept it sternly and solemnly as a*
> *fearful necessity. (Leo Tolstoy, War and Peace)*

Airlift to Sanctuary: One Kiss says a Thousand Words

She was a tiny brown child, terribly thin and tired,
probably only three or four. He was a grizzled,
greying Darwin bus service driver in need of a
shave. He wants to be known only as George. He
doesn't know her name but he'll never forget her.

He saw her walking down the ramp of the
Hercules with one of the first groups flown into
Darwin in the airlift from Dili. Almost all of them
were crying, he noticed. But she knelt and briefly,
gently, kissed the tarmac.

'That's the best thing I've seen,' he says later.
'I've seen it in movies, but I've never seen it in real
life. And, mate, it made me feel real good.'

They had left their homeland... 1544 of them,
under cover of darkness and the taunts of the
Indonesian troops accompanying them. 'Why are
you going to Australia? You have a country yourself,' the soldiers told Nemezia Fernandez.

They waited at the airport until 5 am Dili time,
when the first of the RAAF Hercules began flying

out in what United Nations officials described as an air bridge…

'Since I was on the aircraft I feel that I was free,' says thirty-six-year-old Ms Fernandez. 'I feel like I was walking on the bridge, and below the bridge so many crocodiles.'

When there is a job to be done, it will change perspectives, as Weary Dunlop records:

> In a sense, I am perhaps less a Christian even than I was before the war, but I have been taught very soundly that one must believe in some religion, or sink into the terrible mire of utter selfishness and materialism, so I will always hesitate to say anything against any religion. Man seems to be still far too unintelligent an animal to realise that happiness comes from harmonious relationships with one's fellows and service to mankind rather that in a dirty, unprincipled self-seeking existence.[17]

[1] Hutchinson, p. 2
[2] Rundall, p. 87
[3] Hutchinson, pp. 144–5
[4] Hutchinson, p. 145
[5] Gullett, quoted in Hutchinson, pp. 145–6
[6] Keneally, p. 108
[7] Hutchinson, p. 145
[8] Hutchinson, p. 152
[9] Gullett, H., quoted in Hutchinson, pp. 151-2
[10] Hutchinson, p. 147
[11] Dunlop, p. 264

[12] Dunlop, p. xv
[13] Keneally, et al. p.165
[14] Dunlop, pp. xv–xvi
[15] *The Asialink Centre 1995 to 1997*, Asialink
    Publication p. 11
[16] 'Ordinary Women: Extraordinary Stories', *World
    Vision of Australia* leaflet
[17] Dunlop, p. 178

Seek Beauty

My friend Maurita had arranged everything for the
four of us to attend the Viennese Ball, which was on
the programme of the Festival of Perth. Partners
had been commandeered, tickets bought and we
had made our 19th-century gowns. All that was left
to do was to buy 30 feet of white lace for Maurita's
gown with the voluminous hoop skirt and enormously long hem. She had driven all over Perth
startling shop assistants as she went with her
request. Not surprisingly, no one stocked such a
length of lace. Nevertheless nothing dimmed her
excitement for the night.

A week or so before the big event, Maurita and
her friend taught my partner and I how to do
sweeping circular waltzes around the 'ballroom' at
her place. We got the gist of it but bumped into each
other and a post or two cut our grand circles at
abrupt right angles. It was so much fun and we
knew that a poor rehearsal probably meant a great
performance on the night. Here's hoping.

Lace bought eventually, sewing machine stilled,
we walked into the impressive, 19th-century sand-
stone Fremantle Arts Centre to the strains of Strauss

wafting around and through the dancers' feet. The string orchestra played every waltz tune we knew and we glided across the wooden dance floor, swirling with others dressed like they belonged to another century and another country much older than ours.

Maurita and I had our partners dancing every melody and only stopped when the MC announced that there would be a demonstration of folk dancing in the courtyard. Girls in colourful, embroidered costumes and men in traditional dress enjoyed performing complex dances under the stars.

When we returned inside, supper was being organised: a full meal of several courses, accompanied by heavy silver cutlery. Forming a scalloped effect, chairs were placed in semicircles around the perimeter of the dance floor with a table in each scallop. This arrangement allowed me to talk with those in the adjacent party.

'Oh, I was so looking forward to coming to the ball – couldn't wait. When I heard about it, I immediately sent my daughter out to buy us some tickets. I just love a ball – the dancing and waltzing, all the beautiful music and look at those gorgeous dresses the girls are wearing. It's wonderful!'

The lady loving the evening with such ardent sentiments, wasn't one of the nimble-footed on the floor. She was a quadriplegic in a wheelchair.

Was her enjoyment of the evening dimmed because she couldn't waltz? She gave no indication of this. The night was special for her as well as for me.

Weeks later I attended a music therapy session out of curiosity and found the same woman there. I have used this illustration of the lady who couldn't move but enjoyed dancing so much, many times since then in dance workshops. It proves that the kinaesthetic sense (sense of movement) God has given us, remains with us even though we can't move any more. (How easy but how wrong to assume disabled people wouldn't be interested in a ball.) The evening was feeding her soul even if not her body directly. The music coursed through her veins and she was vicariously moving on the inside and loving it! Isn't God good – he thinks of all eventualities?

The music therapy definitely worked. I wasn't sure what results to expect because I hadn't been to a session before. But I walked out feeling so light – amazingly freed from every stress. All we'd been doing was making improvised music. Isn't God imaginative to create music, enjoyable and rewarding that it is, with the added benefit of relieving stresses?

When I became serious about my Christian walk I looked at how to put into action biblical directives for caring for people. While living in Perth at the time, I was surrounded by Christian people who were greatly involved with community development, social justice issues, urban outreach and the like. I worked for most of my three and a half years in Perth as a youth worker. I tried to do the right thing and be committed to the same things that they

were passionate about. But my heart just wasn't in
it at all and I couldn't work out why. The motives
and theological underpinning of the schemes were
completely sound. I realised over time that just
because they were operating in their calling, it did-
n't mean that I was. It just wasn't my calling. That
left the big blank hole – what was my calling?

I have had an affinity all my life with the visual
and performing arts; they draw me like a magnet.
When I see a fascinating art exhibition or dance performance, everything inside me responds positive-
ly. But when I was caught up in the community
development projects, everything inside me
responded negatively. Somewhere along the road
some cheap thief had whispered in my ear that the
arts were of no 'use' – merely entertainment. It
doesn't help the world in any way, so I felt guilty
putting time and money into the arts. Better to
spend the money on development projects like
other people did and improve the lot of the poor.

By way of analogy, I am reminded of Augustus
Fawnhope in the Georgette Heyer (tongue in cheek)
novel *The Grand Sophy*. While young Amabel is
lying in bed desperately ill and the female members
of the household are attending her day and night
for long weary weeks, Fawnhope instead wrote
poetry about the girl. The poetry seemed to the rest
of the family pointless and totally unhelpful in this
crisis. But he wanted to contribute something to the
situation in a way that was from his heart and used
his ability, his only ability, since other avenues were
closed to him. It's easy to dismiss artistic endeavours for the same reasons, in the face of say, the cry-

ing need for development workers in Third World countries.

However, God's economy is not ours. He uses all our skills (when relinquished to his service) because all our gifts are important to him.

It was glorious the day I realised that God had called all of us to use our talents and abilities, for his purpose and glory for the benefit of humanity. Yes, I know this probably sounds rather obvious to the enlightened. I had heard the sermons for years about using one's talents for God's service. I think one of the reasons why I hadn't understood this biblical message properly was because sermons used examples of talents like hospitality, singing, administration, etc., rather than dancing. That's a recent arrival to ministry in the church though the directive to dance to the Lord was written in the Bible how many thousands of years ago? Read Psalm 149.

No one had told me that I wasn't called to use the gifts I didn't have – especially at the expense of the gifts I did have. In short, this understanding released me from community development projects which were other people's callings, not mine, and into the arts projects that were my calling. Oh bliss, oh rapture! You mean I can dance and not feel guilty? Wow!

The following is an intriguing extract from a devotional book that the authors believed came as a direct revelation from the Lord. It is poignant because the women who wrote the messages lived in desperate poverty and sickness during the Great Depression and yet experienced abundant blessing from intimate communion with the Lord. He commanded them to permeate the brokenness of the world with his love, joy and laughter.

> Draw Beauty from every flower and Joy from the song of the birds, and the colour of the flowers. Drink in the Beauty of air and colour. I am with you. When I wanted to express a beautiful thought, I made a lovely flower. I have told you. Reflect. When I wanted to express to man what I am – what My Father is – I strive to make a very beautiful character. Think of yourselves as My expression of attributes, as a lovely flower is My expression of thought, and you will strive in all, in Spiritual beauty, in Thought-power, in Health, in clothing, to be as fit an expression for Me as you can. Absorb Beauty. As soon as the beauty of a flower or a tree is impressed upon your soul it leaves an image there which reflects through your actions. Remember that no thought of sin and suffering, of the approaching scorn and Crucifixion, ever prevented My seeing the beauty of flowers. Look for beauty and joy in the world around. Look at a flower until its beauty becomes part of your very soul. It will be given back to the world again by you in the form of a smile or a loving word or a kind thought or a prayer. Listen to a bird. Take the song as a message from My Father. Let it sink into your soul. That, too, will be given back to the world in ways I have said. Laugh more, laugh often. Love more. I am with you. I am your Lord.[1]

I find it difficult to reconcile the gruesome, hideous death of Christ and its implications for us, with the breathtaking beauty that God has created in all its forms in the world. Why waste time appreciating nature when there are people dying of starvation or war? Perhaps the writer of this sentence is also seeing the juxtaposition: 'Remember that no thought of sin and suffering, of the approaching scorn and Crucifixion, ever prevented My seeing the beauty of flowers.'

If Jesus can experience the beauty of what his Father created – God's work of art – and also experience what the devil threw at him in all its horror, then we are set free to pursue lives which keep these issues in balance as well. What better way to reflect God's glory than through the arts? Everyone must find his or her own giftings and as much as possible find their callings within those giftings and not accept what others think they should do. The crunch comes when the needs in the community are so pressing and people are pressurising the artist to help in ways which do not express their gifts. Would people understand the word 'no'? Not necessarily. They might misunderstand and use the word 'uncaring'.

God designed his creation with a beauty that would bring restoration to our weary souls and bodies. Our art when under the master's hand frequently touches people in the same way.

Jackie Pullinger who works with drug addicts in Hong Kong, knew a boy called Bibi. 'Into the light slipped a pathetic figure, very very young and very very thin and clearly addicted to heroin.'[2] He des-

perately needed to go into one of the homes Jackie
was linked to in order to come off drugs. But they
were all full to overflowing. Jackie had the unpleasant task of telling him there was no vacancy at the
time; he would have to wait. Bibi raged at her. She
said:

> Just for a moment, Bibi take your eyes off yourself.
> Forget that our house is going to save you. Just look up
> at the sky. It's not a very beautiful sky down in
> Kowloon City … imagine the One who made all of
> that sky, the heavens and the earth and the sea and the
> birds … He chooses that His Spirit should live in us
> rotten as we are. Why? Because Jesus left all that glory
> and walked through the miserable Walled City and
> got beaten up and killed and died and rose again so
> that we could have His Spirit.

It is interesting to see the way the Lord ministered
to him – through a vision of breathtaking loveliness
which was a healing balm to his ravaged body and
mind.

Jackie left him there praying, to talk with another addict and returned half an hour later. She called
to him twice but he would not answer. His eyes
were closed. When he reluctantly opened them on
the third try, she asked him what he saw:

> He told me that he had seen Jesus, at least he thought
> it was Jesus, wearing a long white robe. He had been
> on a mountain and Jesus had come towards him with
> his hand held out; He said to Bibi, 'Bibi, will you fol-
> low me?' Bibi replied, 'Well, yes Lord, who else?' Jesus

had taken him by the hand along the most beautiful path. 'I can hardly describe it.' Bibi searched for words in his meagre experience. 'It was so beautiful. There were lovely flowers and birds and it was very sweet smelling. It was the most lovely place. We walked along this path and I heard you calling but I didn't want to come back.'[3]

A vacancy appeared a day later in one of the homes for him. Bibi always looked to his Creator to solve his problems from that day on rather than the house ministry.

To a young boy who knew little else except the confines and vice of the Walled City of Hong Kong the lesson in who God is, couldn't have been predicted. Another Christian may have prayed that the Lord show him his sin, need of a saviour or teach him ways to get over his hurts. But the Lord knew what his soul was craving and it wasn't a lecture on spirituality.

God took him along a path seeing, smelling and experiencing his creation with the supernatural awareness akin presumably to the way God experiences it. The splendour of it was only sketchily captured in words. Ever stood on a mountaintop and seen a panoramic vista or a painting or a ballet that moved you almost to tears by its beauty or depth of meaning? Ever felt that your senses were not keen enough to take in what you see?

You know that the genius of God's brush-stroke has reached out and touched your soul in places rarely touched. Albert Schweitzer gave himself fully to the rapture of wonderful music. Once as a boy, while standing outside his classroom he heard some boys singing Alsatian folk songs in two-part harmony for the first time. He said that he had to steady himself on the wall nearby, so 'over-whelmed' was he by such ecstasy.

Somehow sadly you know that God is seeing the scene in an infinitely richer way than you ever could on this earth. But then there are heaven's panoramas, pictures and dances and we will enjoy them for an eternity… with the eyes of heaven, just as our past loved ones are enjoying them at this moment.

For Albert nature was joyously evocative. To the American biographer Hermann Hagedorn, he recalled:

> Even when I was a child I was like a person in an ecstasy in the presence of Nature, without anyone sus-pecting it. I consider Nature as the great consoler. In her I always found calm and serenity again when I was disturbed. And this has only become accentuated during the course of my life … Unforgettable pictures of the country are engraved on my memory. I roam among these memories as in a gallery in which are hung the most beautiful landscapes painted by the greatest masters … It is said I am a man of action. But at bottom I am a dreamer, and it is in reveries, reviving the living contact with Nature, that I gather the pow-ers that make me an active being.[4]

His last message is the lesson that all overtaxed church workers need to hear. Too much pain com-ing into our lives and not enough beauty makes the burden far too heavy for us. No wonder Jesus used to wander over the mountains when he needed to recharge his spiritual batteries through communion with his father.

Likewise, Bibi was forever changed from that moment when God invited him to see the majesty of his creation. Appreciating God's masterpiece gives answers to the questions and doubts that lurk in our minds. Seeing the infinite size of God puts our mountainous problems into their proper perspective as minor hiccups or distractions from his plans.

When I consider Your heavens, the work of Your fingers, the moon and the stars, which You have ordained, what is man that you are mindful of Him, and the son of man that You visit him? (Ps. 8:3–4)

David was marvelling at the moon and stars, but Milford Sound in New Zealand makes one ask the same question: 'What is man that you are mindful of Him?' Who am I? Why did you provide such magnificent country for sinful humanity?

Kiwis know about mountains. They know the difference between molehills and soaring ranges. Most of Australia's mountains are just blips on the horizon compared to New Zealand's Mt Cook (3753 m), Mt Aspiring (3027 m); the list goes on. Milford Sound in Fiordland on the South Island can make the proudest person know his/her size and importance in the world. The pinnacles forming Milford Sound are so massive they throw out one's

estimation of distance from point A to point B. Tour
guides on the cruise down the Sound take delight in
asking passengers to estimate the distance from the
boat to a waterfall gushing into the river.
Everyone's answers woefully underestimate the
mark.

My friend Frances and I had seen the travel photos of Mitre Peak rising dramatically out of the deep
waters on cloudless days. But when we actually
stood on the banks at the right location to see it for
ourselves, we looked at all the mountains, looked at
each other and whispered: 'Which one is it?' (How
can you lose a mountain that is right in front of
you?) Perhaps the clouds obscured the peak. New
Zealand is called the Land of the Long White Cloud
for good reason. It wasn't an anti-climax, the view
was still awe-inspiring without the bright sunlight
the poster had promised.

God spoke to me a different message through the
presence of another impressive range – the
Remarkables near Lake Wakatipu and Queenstown
in the same part of southern New Zealand. He set
me up well for this encounter.

My second trip to the country was to work with
a dance teacher in Dunedin. But I yearned to revis-
it Queenstown and see the picturesque countryside
there. It just so happened that the sister of the
woman I was boarding with lived near
Queenstown and she just happened to come to
Dunedin and was travelling back home the next
day and yes, there was room in the ... I was first in
the car. On the long journey I was excited to see
snow on the peaks glowing faintly in the moonlight

as we neared our destination. But nothing prepared me for what awaited me in daylight.

Next morning I woke up and opened the drapes on the broad windows. The view of the Remarkables flooded my consciousness and God thundered in my spirit: I made these mountains. I have no idea how long I stood there fixed to the spot. God suddenly became personal as he shared with me his handiwork.

> *Be still and know that I am God;*
> *I will be exalted among the nations,*
> *I will be exalted in the earth. (Ps. 46:10)*

I saw the outpouring of his power and creative ability. The biblical writers had had similar encounters with God's awesome strength and creative energy when they realised God could produce mountains, make them melt, drown or move them into the sea if he wanted them to. Amazing! How could I ever consider any problem outside the Almighty's hand to overcome after experiencing this message? The Remarkables are a constant reminder when I doubt. The memory of seeing billions of tonnes of rocks and dirt heaped up in spectacular forms and remembering his message always humbles me. 'Yes I think you can handle my problems Lord!'

> *He made the earth by His power;*
> *He has established the world by His wisdom,*
> *And stretched out the heaven by His understanding.*
> *When He utters His voice*
> *There is a multitude of waters in the heavens:*

*He causes the vapors to ascend from the ends of
the earth;
He makes lightnings for the rain;
He brings the wind out of His treasures.
(Jer. 51:15–16)*

Since God made the earth by his power, wisdom
and understanding, could it be when we meditate
on all he created and seek him for guidance and
solutions to problems, that he imparts to us his
power, wisdom and understanding, in short all we
need?

> Doing what God calls us to do, that's what success is.
> Often that means flogging the flesh as God wants to
> bring us out of what's comfortable. God constantly
> humbles me. Just when I have a handle on things, he
> shows me a bigger view.[5]

Taking views is Ken Duncan's business and ministry. He is one of Australia's principal landscape
photographers and one of the world's leading
panoramic specialists. His photographs capture the
essence of the variety of our country's natural beauty. At his three galleries in Sydney and Melbourne,
Ken displays one of his beloved passages of scripture:

*For since the creation of the world, God's invisible qual-
ities – his eternal power and divine nature – have been
clearly seen, being understood from what has been
made, so that men are without excuse.
(Rom. 1:20; NIV)*

I had a chance to see two of his photographs at close range. He donated them for a fund-raising auction and dinner organised to support the outreach arm of my church. Yes, they would have done very nicely in my lounge room. Sadly, someone else came to the same conclusion.

Faith is at the centre of Ken's life and work but it hadn't always been that way. Three incidents made him realise he needed to reach out to God. The first time he was on a trip to Central Australia. At the time he was experimenting with Aboriginal Dreamtime (traditional beliefs) and was attacked spiritually. He cried out to God to rescue him.

The second occasion he developed gangrene and had to have half a toe amputated. The third time he was run down by hypothermia in Tasmania. Three months after he recovered he and his wife Pamela gave their hearts to the Lord.

He believes his book *America Wide: In God we Trust* is part of God's vision to bring Americans back to an awareness of God's sovereignty. This theme was demonstrated graphically while in Colorado when he tried to capture on film a carpet of wildflowers in the mountains. It rained. It rained for two hours. Then he prayed, 'Lord, if you could just part these clouds, and if the sun were to come through, we would have a great shot.'

Thunder crashed and rain pelted harder than ever. But Ken remained firm in his faith. Then the sun broke through the clouds and a rainbow hung across the mountains and valley abundant with wildflowers. Ken said the photo was a gift from God. Another photographer told Ken that he was 'lucky'. Ken said: 'Mate, that was not luck, that was God.'[6]

The photograph is stunning and well worth the wait.

Albert Schweitzer experienced pain and beauty. As a sensitive child and adult, who didn't wear filters across his ears or eyes, he felt keenly the pain of the people and animals around him. In a strange twist of providence, when he and his wife Hélène were interned during World War One, they stayed in St Remy, a place famous for another occupant generations before. He recalled:

> The first time I entered the big room on the ground floor which was our day-room, it struck me as being, in its unadorned and bare ugliness, strangely familiar. Where, then, had I seen that iron stove, and the flue-pipe crossing the room from end to end? They mystery was solved at last; I knew them from a drawing of Van Gogh's. The building in which we were housed, once a monastery in a walled-up garden, had till recently been occupied by sufferers from nervous or mental diseases. Among them at one time was Van Gogh, who immortalised with his pencil the desolate room in which today we in our turn were sitting about. Like us, he had suffered from the cold floor when the Mistral blew! Like us, he had walked round and round between the high garden walls![7]

One could only speculate why the Lord would allow such a coincidence. Was there a lesson in the life of Van Gogh which Albert and Hélène needed to learn? To see the divine connection between pain and beauty as represented in the vivid paintings and tragic life of Vincent Van Gogh? Did one rely on the other in some way? Did feeling one enhance the experience of the other?

Albert Schweitzer was an accomplished concert organist with a passion for the music of Johann Sebastian Bach. Giving concert recitals partly paid for their voyage to Africa. On their circuitous route to Gabon (formerly French Equatorial Africa), they visited St Sulpice in Paris where Albert played the organ for the last time on Easter Sunday. The Paris Bach Society gave him a surprise present of a piano in appreciation of his many years as their organist. The piano had organ pedals and was housed in a lead-lined crate.

I love this story because it shows so clearly God honouring the enormous sacrifice and risk that Albert and Hélène were making, especially given the year, 1913. There were not many modern appliances in the jungle then. Pioneers in those days gave themselves to the field for life, not just a term of a year or two. He was giving up the investment of many years of learning and polishing the art so dear to his heart, and instead treating patients in the heart of Gabon. But God knew the loss and wanted to reward him in a way which would also relieve the pressures he was to feel in Africa.

So often people edge away from overtures to enter mission enterprises because they are so afraid that they wouldn't be able to do all the things on the mission field that they enjoy at home.

The underlying fear is that God is a miser who wants to take and not give. Secondly, that God will expect the exercise of abilities which are not inherent in the person, while denying abilities which are already developed. For example, Albert never to play music again once he entered the forests of Gabon.

In my experience the exact reverse is the case: to stay at home is to live the restricted life. Once I was on the field, I realised that all through my life the Lord had been training me, developing my abilities 'for such a time as this' cf. Esther 4:14b. What a privilege! Missionaries to their amazement often discover new gifts within them and God provides openings to develop these gifts then use them to bless other people. Sometimes it takes a mission term, long or short, to unearth the treasure inside. Extraordinary fulfilment is found when a life is lived exercising all one's skills and talents in the service of others. In the case of Albert Schweitzer his life clearly showed the interplay of all his interests and study in serving Africans. Is it any wonder that in old age when his friends urged him to retire to the comfort of Europe that he refused, preferring to end his days aged ninety, in his beloved Lambaréné?

In mission ventures God ties the many skills of people into a team effort. He knows what he is doing when he puts a team together. Members see that what comes to fruition is the culmination of all the innate abilities and training he has provided over the years, married to individual desires and interests.

I wonder if, when God sees a new recruit touch the soil of his or her adoptive country, he thinks with great satisfaction: 'That's my woman, that's my man I've been nurturing and training for the past 2, (30 or 40) years waiting for this moment.'

The wobbling knees belong to someone feeling it's the first day at kindergarten, but to God they have reached a major milestone.

One person who has passed a milestone in her professional and spiritual life is Dot Wilkin of Sydney, Australia. Dot realised while at Bible College that her painting was a spiritual gift. She explained in an interview with *Alive* magazine:

> Just as Bezalel and Oholiab were called to make artworks in the book of Exodus, God calls us to serve with all our gifts. Through self-denial, God showed me that my art was not only a talent, but a spiritual gifting. I was convicted that it was going to be used more powerfully in the future.[8]

This prophecy was confirmed on 8 April 1998 when she was awarded third place in the inaugural Great Southland Exhibition and Art Prize. ('The Great Southland of the Holy Spirit' was the name given to Australia by one of our earliest explorers.) She was subsequently asked to exhibit with other winners in Parliament House, Canberra, in November of that year.

I'm really into symbolism. I'll look at a waratah [large, flaming-red flower native to Australia] in the bush and be struck by the way it springs from a black, burnt-out tree. It's like new life springing forth in the bush. I'll then incorporate that with ancient symbols.[9]

Dot studied ancient Christian iconography at university. Past Christians used the symbols to convey explanations of Scripture and to communicate and encourage one another during persecution.

The abstract and spiritual aspects of symbolic shapes have always intrigued me and that's why I use them in my art. I have researched and become absorbed in them with expression, colour and texture.[10]

In October 1999 Dot held her first solo exhibition at the NSW Parliament which she entitled 'Advent'.

With the use of ancient Christian and Australian symbolism, Dot expounded scripture to communicate that God is the beginning and the end, the reconciliator who has come to heal Australia, its people and government. Dot explains that she is not wanting fame and fortune but rather: 'It's quite simply that I believe this is what God wants me to do. The goal of my art is to edify and draw people to God.'[11]

What a great goal. She mentioned the down side, especially the high expense of exhibiting. But obedience to what she believed the Lord wanted for her life had its own rewards in terms of exposure of her passion for faith and art to a wider audience than she could have imagined when starting out painting as a young girl.

Colours of Christmas

'You know of course that the colours of Christmas aren't green and bright red, they are purple, scarlet, white and blue.'

'Oh yes, um, of course.' I can't quite remember what I said, or muttered, not wanting to show my ignorance. This comment intrigued me. I wanted to know if what my friend said had any currency. A bit of investigation produced the following. (Correct me if I am wrong.)

In the British tradition, I gleaned that green stands for green growth – leaves, trees, etc. Red represents the red berries on holly that appear around Christmastime in the Northern Hemisphere. Holly also grows in Australia. I pinched some from next door once for our Christmas table. (It was legal because it was overhanging the street!) I don't recall seeing red berries though. But the biblical symbolism for purple, scarlet, blue and white carries a rich embroidery of meaning:

1. Purple – royalty, dominion, power, first of the King of kings and second, of those who are called to rule and reign with him.
2. Scarlet – the colour of blood refers to self-denial and sacrifice, especially the sacrifice of the cross; something we too are called to share in.

3. Blue – heavenly and peaceful. First, the heavenly origin of the Prince of Peace and second, if we are to have peace we must set our affections on things above.

Scarlet and blue mix together to produce purple. Therefore when there is a mix of heavenly mind-edness with a willingness to sacrifice, we emerge with regal glory and dominion, walking in our kingship and calling as sons [and daughters] of God.[12]

I know which tradition has the most meaningful symbolism in it for me and which one pales into insignificance by comparison and it doesn't have come-and-go berries in it. Food for thought around Christmas, isn't it?

The Story of the Praying Hands

The author of this story is unknown but is quoted by Gray in *Stories for the Heart*.

About 1490 two young friends, Albrecht Dürer and Franz Knigstein, were struggling young artists. Since both were poor, they worked to support themselves while they studied art.

Work took so much of their time and advancement was slow. Finally, they reached an agreement: they would draw lots, and one of them would work to support both of them while the other would study art. Albrecht won and began to study, while Franz worked at hard labour to support them. They agreed that when Albrecht was successful he would support Franz who would then study art.

Albrecht went off to the cities of Europe to study. As the world now knows, he had not only talent but genius. When he had attained success, he went back to keep his bargain with Franz. But Albrecht soon discovered the enormous price his friend had paid. For as Franz worked at hard manual labour to support his friend, his fingers had become stiff and twisted. His slender, sensitive hands had been ruined for life. He could no longer execute the delicate brush strokes necessary for fine painting. Though his artistic dreams could never be realised, he was not embittered but rather rejoiced in his friend's success.

One day Dürer came upon his friend unexpectedly and found him kneeling with his gnarled hands intertwined in prayer, quietly praying for the success of his friend although he himself could no longer be an artist. Albrecht Dürer, the great genius, hurriedly sketched the folded hands of his faithful friend and later completed a truly great masterpiece known as *The Praying Hands*.

Today art galleries everywhere feature Albrecht Dürer's works, and this particular masterpiece tells an eloquent story of love, sacrifice, labour and gratitude. It has reminded multitudes around the world of how they may also find comfort, courage and strength.

Who could have foreseen that the giving of my dance ability to the Lord would have transported

me to China year after year? Where would I have
gone if I had stayed in youth work and community
development? I would definitely have burnt out
years before because I wasn't specifically gifted
for that type of work. Instead I was part of a team
that has performed on stages to audiences ranging
from a small gathering to almost four thousand
people. It's amazing why the Chinese see us as anything different to what we are, an ordinary bunch of
people, warts and all. We saw this disparity very
clearly when we performed in an isolated city a few
years back.

'I think I love you, so what am I so afraid of?' The
words were ringing out at that time in seventies
revival rock 'n roll. The place was alive with 2500
people screaming excitedly. In another decade
political speeches below the huge People's Republic
of China symbol reverberated throughout the place,
fervently stirring the shouts of the audience.

We were in a town nestled amongst the soaring
karst mountains that sprang out of the landscape
like witches hats all over the region and parts of
neighbouring provinces. The area was on our
packed tour of schools and universities in southern
provinces. As well as performing, we taught
English classes in each place we visited. The exertions of scrimping and raising money with chocolate drives and a hike-athon for the fare to China
were behind the team now. We performed free of
charge for our audiences. The previous night's concert was for the staff and students of the senior high
school (all two thousand of them). During the day
at the school, the team had taught English, talked

about Australia and chatted with students eager to learn about other countries. This night was different because it was open to the general public.

'It feels weird, they treat us like pop stars, but we're just ordinary people,' commented Sally, a physiotherapist in her 'normal' life. Tonight she danced, sang and played keyboard and wondered why people were making such a fuss of her.

The band switched to a bouncy Chinese folk tune and the performers danced an energetic bush-dance with Chinese ribbons making effervescent curlicues in the air during the slower musical interludes. The audience responded with surprised laughter to see their own cultural forms used by these strange-looking westerners. The town is in a remote corner; a province away from big cities and contact with westerners. Distant also from some of the dominant nationality, the Han Chinese, because much of the population are from a minority group.

Our motley bunch of performers was the first live western band to play in the town. Some of our songs they knew, others are golden oldies, but are new to them and a few were written by two of the singers.

The deep, resonant tones of 'Jailhouse Rock' were the cues for Mark and myself to come on stage for a 1950s rock 'n roll dance. The audience vicariously loved the flirting, flings in the air and frenzied speed of the dance. The antics of one-up-man-ship by the singers in the breaks of 'Long Tall Glasses' were enjoyed by all.

'*Ni xianzai hai hao ma? Shi fou guo zhe ni xiang yao de sheng huo.*'

The place erupted as the people realised that David was singing in Chinese. Standing, cheering, running to the foot of the stage with hands raised, the young people pressed against each other for a closer look.

'I'm on the top of the world, looking down on creation.' Young girls joined Sally in singing this song; an everlasting favourite with students all over China. Walking near the edge of the stage, admirers jostled to reach her. She shook hands with a lad who tugged too eagerly and she staggered forward. We chose 1970s numbers for the tour because they have strong rhythms, are easily sung by English language students and suit their taste in popular music. Patriotic hands clapped as I reproduced Chinese gestures in a rhythmic dance to the song:

> *Rivers, mountains in my dreams, my homeland*
> *calls to me,*
> *Though I've not been there for so many years, this*
> *won't change my Chinese heart.*
> *The Great Yangzi, the Great Wall and Yellow River*
> *always on my mind,*
> *No matter where I am, no matter when, they are in*
> *my heart.*

Screaming and waving, the audience sang along with the chorus sung in Chinese. Soon it was time for:

> *With tears in your eyes you might say goodbye,*
> *Holding hands that don't want to let go.*

As he sang the last note, David ran behind the stage gathering the rest of us in his wake. The crowd was densest in front and he saw youngsters being crushed against the front of the stage by older ones behind them. In such a vast audience charged with excitement, the atmosphere quivered with the possibility of serious injury. The police immediately sprang to disperse the people as quickly as possible. But people just stood around wanting to soak up the last of the magic of the evening. We waited for the electric atmosphere to abate a little.

Emerging after a few minutes, we started packing up the gear. Cameras clicked in all directions and some of the young people were allowed to come through the police barrier at the stage doors to meet us. Excitedly they pulled us into position and more cameras flashed.

All night we had been wondering what the Party Secretary and his colleagues were thinking as they sat alone in the shadows in the wings opposite our side. A good sign was that we were allowed to perform at all, after last night. The second concert was toned down just in case. But we need not have worried, he was all smiles and actually patted me on the shoulder after the concert, rather an un-Chinese thing to do!

Instead of going home, the crowd had surrounded the hall exits outside. We piled the gear near the back-stage door. The police unlocked the door and held the crowd back as we carried the equipment through to a waiting van. The girls jumped in and sat on top of the gear. The van slowly parted the people who were waving, cheering and passing notes and gifts to us through the windows. The guys walked to the hostel just down the road.

The night was reminiscent of the Beatles' era when teenagers reacted to a new kind of music. Now I know how scary a huge excitable audience can be. Yes, Sally it is weird. Do we really look that strange?

---

[1] Russell, p. 70
[2] Pullinger and Quicke, p. 194
[3] Pullinger and Quicke, pp. 199–200
[4] Schweitzer, A., in Brabazon, p. 27
[5] Atkins, p. 20
[6] Atkins, p. 20
[7] Memorial Article to Archbishop Nathan Söderblom May 1933, in Brabazon, pp. 272–3
[8] Wilkin, D., quoted in Smith, p. 28
[9] Wilkin, D., quoted in Smith, p. 28
[10] Wilkin, D., quoted in Smith, p. 28
[11] Wilkin, D., quoted in Smith, p. 28
[12] Shreve, p. 281
[13] Gray, p. 271

9

Never See an Evil

Never see an evil without trying to find a remedy.
(Motto of Mary Mackillop, Mother Mary of the Cross,
1842–1909)

These words were spoken by Mary Mackillop, lived out in her life and seen in the devotion of the sisters of the Order of the Sisters of St Joseph of the Sacred Heart which she founded. They guided her when she travelled thousands of kilometres to outback Australia and New Zealand founding homes for the disadvantaged and schools for the poor. Her witness was rewarded posthumously in January 1995 when His Holiness Pope John Paul II made her a saint.

From the reading I had done of her experiences, I became increasingly drawn to know more about her. 'Sainthood' is hardly a term Australians use every day. We think of saints as people who lived hundreds of years ago – in Europe. One day while rummaging through a pile of second-hand books in an opportunity shop looking for a maths book, I discovered, lo and behold, a copy of *The Official Mackillop Papal Visit Book 1995*. It outlined the pro-

gramme of the Pope's visit including the beatifica-
tion ceremony and his private visit to her tomb at
Mount Street, Sydney. There was also the history of
Mary Mackillop. Her life story contains many fascinating lessons for people from every denomination.
To give the modern day Catholic Church credit, the
authorised biography, *An Extraordinary Australian:
Mary Mackillop*, written by Paul Gardiner S.J. contains an honest and detailed account of her remarkable life and hides nothing about the ungodly
behaviour by some clergy who tried to rule her
order.

> Mary had all the qualities that Australians admire. She
> had the 'human touch' and treated people as if they
> were special. She had patience and goodness in times
> of personal hardship. Her abilities to cope with diffi-
> culties without being discouraged and the way she
> was able to find a solution to problems made others
> around her want to do the same. Throughout all her
> work, the love she felt for others was due to her com-
> plete faith in and love for God.[1]

Today near St Patrick's Cathedral and St Vincent's
Hospital, Melbourne is a plaque in the footpath:
'On this site Mary Mackillop, Foundress of the
Sisters of St Joseph was born on 15th January, 1842.'

Named Maria Ellen, the eldest child of
Alexander and Flora Mackillop, she was born soon
after they migrated from Scotland (Lochaber and
Glenfinnen respectively) and married in
Melbourne. (Merino Cottage her first home is no
longer there. Three months after she was born, the

cottage was sold due to financial problems. Today on the same site is the Mary Mackillop Pilgrimage Centre.) Symbolic of the family's future, dogged by poverty, was the wedding ceremony in 1840. Too poor for a proper ring, Alexander made one instead by punching out a circle from a gold sovereign.

It was through the poverty brought about by the trials of a large family coping with business and other failures, that the gold in Mary's character was forged. She grew to be a woman of determination, compassion, bravery, honesty, courage and humility. She identified with the suffering of the poor so much so that, even during her formative years, she conceived the idea of setting up schools for under-privileged children. Fortunately for Mary, unusual in her time and social situation, her parents were both educated and so they taught their children how to read and write.

She once expressed her vision for the St Joseph schools as: '...humble. [They are] intended only for the poor and have nothing to do with the great and learned.'[2]

Other religious orders of the time taught young people from the middle and upper classes in large convents, so her idea of providing for the education of the poor was exceedingly revolutionary for her era.

At fourteen she went to Penola in South Australia to become a governess to the ten children of her Aunt Margaret Cameron. Alexander Cameron was 'king' in the district with a property of 15,000 ha. It was here in a new life, surrounded by comparative wealth, that she dreamed of schools in remote areas. She wanted to provide opportunities for neglected, working class children to learn to read and write, be fed and to live in better circumstances.

She put this purpose into practice by helping a neglected part-aboriginal girl, Nancy Bruce. She combed out the lice in her hair, nursed her sores and gave her lessons just as she did for all the underprivileged children on the farm. This care was unusual; normally such attention wasn't common for girls to give to the lower classes in the 1860s.

It was in Penola she met Father Julian Tenison Woods who was to have an enormous influence for better or for worse on her ministry. He suggested they develop an Australian version of a French order of nuns who ran schools for poor children in France.

After two years in Penola, she was no longer needed, so became a governess in Portland to 14 Cameron cousins. There she passed a teaching examination and started teaching at the Portland Catholic Denominational School. She had found her niche: she loved teaching and life in the church. Her two sisters Maggie and Annie assisted in the school.

A way was opened for teaching in Penola with 35 children in 1865. The building used as the first St Joseph's school was a rough, converted stable. How fitting it was in a stable that the order started, since the nuns strove to meet the needs of the poor and humble children of the district. It reminds us of the birthplace of the one Mary served. Today the location is the Mary Mackillop Memorial Park.

Fr Woods had the task of organising the schools as the Director of Catholic Education in SA. Bishop

Shiel went to Penola from Adelaide to bless her with the title 'Sister Mary'. Other girls wanting to live the simple life of service had already joined Mary. In 1865 with the permission of the Bishop, Woods brought Mary and a new recruit to Adelaide. An Irishwoman – Josephine MacMullen – joined the group and offered her cottage which became the first Josephite community. Not wanting to waste any time, the week they arrived in Adelaide, the sisters started a school in St Francis Xavier's Cathedral hall and enrolments grew rapidly. The timetable included prayers and hymns. Sisters quickly found clothing for children without suitable clothes for school.

The sisters lived the Rule of Life written by Woods which would become a contentious issue in the future. It stated that the sisters must consider themselves poor and the least among all religious orders. They could not own any property and had to beg for all their provision. This sounds most harsh by our standards but Mary and Fr Woods thought in the same vein as St Francis of Assisi. They believed that to be able to identify with the poor then they must have a lifestyle of poverty. They feared that material property would be a snare for the sisters, deflecting them from their work.

Challenging isn't it? God brings into our lives situations which are analogous to the situations and problems of those we are ministering to. But in the order, that close identification was incorporated into the Rule. There is nothing more attractive to a person ardently seeking the Lord's will for her life, than to see another woman living out the truths of the gospel in a simple lifestyle, in the midst of a society struggling in difficult days.

The sticking point became the clause in the Rule that they must operate independently of bishops. This was included for practical reasons. Fr Woods and Mary thought with the huge distances between the towns and cities in Australia, if the order came under the authority of local bishops, then they would impose their own rules and thereby destroy uniformity of operations across the nation. The head sister was to be answerable to Rome only. It was to be hoped priests and bishops would not interfere but history proved the reverse.

On 15 August 1867 at the age of twenty-five Mary took her final vows as Mary of the Cross. Now she was able to serve God and do the works that were desperately needed. She wanted to create opportunities for neglected children to learn to read, write and have enough to eat and live in better conditions.

By July 1868 there were 30 sisters in eight new schools, an orphanage and a home for women in 'moral danger' known as 'The Refuge'. Even so there were many people still left homeless on the streets because welfare was non-existent before the 1900s.

Despite the austerity of the Rule, the order experienced rapid growth. Within three years over 80 women were in training under Mary and requests from pastors for communities to staff their schools flowed in.

The 80 were sent to 30 schools in Adelaide and surrounding towns, the St Vincent de Paul Orphanage and two homes for the homeless in Adelaide. Their refuge for neglected children and women was a new idea and the only one in the city. They took in prostitutes, those with criminal convictions or those running away from violent husbands. These days battered women go to women's refuges, elderly people to elderly care hostels, etc. The different groups are segregated according to age and gender. The Josephite Providence reflected society better by placing women and children together. The name Providence was chosen because the sisters relied entirely on the Lord to provide for their financial needs. Extra expenses for the sisters were the frequent funerals for people who died at the homes. In 1869 the sisters opened The Solitude for the aged, terminally ill and alcoholics.

Nonetheless despite these calls on their services by pastors, the sisters frequently experienced severe financial hardship – often they survived on treacle and bread. They were not readily understood or approved of by their relatives. Sisters were also sent to isolated towns. To the shock of respectable society, they visited criminals and drunks. Such an 'unlady-like' thing to do but to the sisters everyone was equal in their sight. The Josephite Order brought to Australian society a fresh wave of social conscience and the people were both disapproving of their behaviour but at the same time, their hard work, success and dedication were plainly evident.

Mary was fully aware of the enormous changes that living in a convent meant, especially for young sisters. She knew all the girls by name and would write to them regularly, encouraging them through their fears. 'She was generous with her praise and gentle with her reprimands, and demanded no less of herself than she did of others.'[3]

Sister Mary Placid recalled a couple of stories about Mary's kindness to her girls:

> When I was a young professed Sister, another young Sister and I were sent to the country. The train left about 7 pm and we would not reach our destination until about 11 pm. We left Mount Street [convent in Sydney] without tea; somehow Mother found out. A few minutes before the train left, Mother Mary arrived almost breathless with some lunch in a paper bag, and some fruit. When she saw our distress at her coming, she smiled gaily and said she could not have her children without anything to eat until after 11 o'clock.[4]

Another time Mary travelled three hundred kilometres to comfort a dying sister in Port Augusta, who had been badly burnt in an accident with a kerosene lamp. In excruciating pain, the woman had been constantly asking for Mary. She set out from Adelaide at once in a private coach which was the only transport available at that time of day. But she only reached Mt Remarkable, about 60 kilometres short of her destination, and could not find a willing coach driver. Mary walked into a hotel and said: 'Gentlemen, my Sister at Port Augusta is dying, and is constantly asking for me. If one of you will lend me a horse, I will ride there.' Chivalry was not quite dead in those Celtic hearts. Two or three jumped up, got a pair of spanking horses and a buggy, and drove her on that afternoon, where she was in time to console the dying sister.[5]

Their habit was most unsuitable for Australian climatic conditions. The 'Brown Joeys' wore a brown, woollen dress over unbleached calico, dark stockings and black boots. The calico would have been itchy in the height of summer and so hot! Ugh.

In 1870 Mary arrived in Brisbane at the invitation of James Quinn, the Bishop of Brisbane, who asked her to open new schools there. In Queensland Mary saw a group of outcasts, Aborigines and South Sea Islanders – Kanakas. In the 1860s they had provided cheap labour for the cane-growing areas. The Kanakas lived under slave conditions and had come to Australia through kidnapping ('black-birding'). By 1890, fifty thousand of them had arrived in Queensland. Mary and her sisters ran evening classes in English for them and treated them with the same respect as any other people.

At one point she was urged by Dr Cani the Vicar General in Brisbane (in the absence of Bishop Quinn) to accept a government grant for her schools. But there were conditions attached concerning the standard curricula, textbooks and restrictions on religious content in the teaching. At the time it was the policy of the Brisbane diocese to accept government grants and abide with these strictures.

Mary stated her opinion with forthrightness: 'My position as Guardian of our Holy Rule enforces this and in the presence of God I must say what the voice of conscience and duty dictate. It is impossible for us to become in any way connected with Government and be true to the spirit as well as the letter of our Rule.'[6] My, she didn't mince words, did she? (Dr Cani was probably acting under orders from Bishop Quinn. Dr Cani later sent money to the sisters and occasionally organised fund raising for them.)

When the Bishop heard of her reaction, he thought of her as being obstinate and disobedient. He was not pleased. Other teaching orders were not pleased.

Within three months of the arrival of Mary and some Josephite sisters, they opened three schools with three hundred pupils. Clearly other orders were jealous of the popularity of the new Josephites as they lost pupils to them. They feared losing their government grants.

Back in Adelaide criticism of Fr Woods for incompetence and financial mismanagement were thrown in the press and the reluctance of some parish priests to give up their government grants caused much discord. When Mary returned to Adelaide, she was met with the call to close her order down completely.

Shiel, the Bishop of Adelaide had been in Rome, everyone presumed to present the Rule to the Pope. But he refused. When he returned to Adelaide in 1871 he dealt with the controversy by trying to bring the order to heel by dividing it. He dismissed Fr Woods and wanted any sister who did not agree with his changes to the Rule, to be dispensed from their vows. Mary pleaded with him to reconsider the changes and said that what he was doing was against the Rule. All this politicking must be seen against the extent of the work of the sisters: 127 of them teaching in 34 schools at this time.

Bishop Shiel was easily swayed by any stronger personality trying to persuade him. He had a long-standing illness and mental aberrations so was easily led by younger clergy. This explains his earlier pleasure in the expansion of the order and later his severe step of excommunicating Mary.

Bishop Goold commented from Melbourne: 'Poor Dr Shiel, he must labour under mental disease.'[7] The excommunication was the result of misunderstandings and the delivery of wrong messages, not just the machinations of meddling clergy.

Shiel stated: 'On account of your disobedience and rebellion, I pronounce on you the awful sentence of excommunication. You are now Mary Mackillop free to return to the world, a large part of the wickedness of which I am afraid you have brought with you into the Institute.'

Mary's mother Flora responded swiftly: 'I was under the impression that only notorious sinners could be excommunicated ... That she, my ever good child, could be such it is hard for me to believe ... In my opinion, the great sin of her life had been leaving me and putting herself under your Lordship's protection.'

She didn't mince words either!

Wonderful are the words of Mary about the fiasco. She said:

'I really felt like one in a dream. I seemed not to realize the presence of the Bishop and priests; I know I did

not see them; but I felt, oh, such a love for their office,
a love, a sort of reverence for the very sentence which
I then knew was being in full force passed upon me. I
do not know how to describe the feeling, but I was
intensely happy and felt nearer to God than I had ever
felt before. The sensation of the calm, beautiful presence of God I shall never forget.'[8]

Still Mary wept many tears over the closure of the
work which was so dear to her heart and to the sisters. She did not request that the ban be lifted but
accepted it as the will of God for her life. She wanted to forgive everyone who had wronged her. In
this regard she was standing on the word of God
which states that the battle isn't ours it is the Lord's.
He is the one who vindicates us when we are
wronged.

Just before Bishop Shiel's death his mind cleared
and he realised that people had deceived him. In
February 1872 he received the Last Rites while he
was staying in Willunga, 50 kilometres away from
Adelaide. He told Fr Hughes to find Mary and lift
the censure on her. Mary happened to be travelling
from Adelaide to Willunga at the time. An excited
Fr Hughes met her on the road and told her the
good news. He officially absolved her during a ceremony in a Morphett Vale church. In March the sisters renewed their vows.

Through all the troubles of the dark days, Mary
and her beloved sisters were attacked by opponents, yet supported by a few friends among the
clergy and laity. One of her ardent friends was
Joanna Barr-Smith. She and her husband Robert,

though Protestants, were generous financial supporters.

Emmanuel Solomon, a Jewish merchant and Member of Parliament also provided for the sisters. He gave a row of cottages rent-free on several occasions to accommodate them during the early days in Adelaide. Following Mary's excommunication, the sisters could not remain in their accommodation in King William Street, Adelaide.

But now what was needed was approval of the order from Rome, so to be free of domination by local Bishops who had wanted to put restrictions of their laws of poverty and central government. The following year, dressed in plain clothes for protection, Mary went to Rome.

In her letter to Pope Pius IX she stated:

> It is an Australian who writes... The sisters teach the children of the poor for the most part emigrants from the British Isles and other parts of Europe, or children who have been brought up with little knowledge of their religion. It is in a missionary spirit of poverty that the sisters hold themselves ready to go wherever obedience or the cause of the dear little ones of the church demands.[9]

The Pope received Mary twice in 1874. When the Pope blessed her, he gave approval of the Sisters of St Joseph of the Sacred Heart. He agreed to the central government clause, freeing them from bishopric control but made some changes. The sisters could now own property, this was for their own safety and they could own a motherhouse.

Fr Tappeiner replaced Fr Woods as the director of the sisters and Mary became their superior general. She was overjoyed by the outcome even though it had taken almost two years to gain.

Bishops Matthew and James Quinn (brothers) of Bathurst in NSW and QLD respectively still clung to the notion that the sisters in their states must come under their authority. They refused because it was against their Rule, so they left Bathurst. James Quinn expelled them from QLD in 1879.

In 1880 new schools and a Providence were opened in Sydney and outlying areas at the request of Bishop Vaughan who had no desire to control the sisters. Unfortunately Vaughan died soon after this. There was opposition in 1883 with criticism over spending money unwisely and alcoholism. (Mary took a little brandy on the advice of her doctor for a painful condition.) But the demands of the poor for shelter and food continued to mount. Mother Bernard Walsh replaced Mary as superior general: a decision Mary took courageously. But 1883 saw growth in the work with the opening of schools and refuges in Temuka, New Zealand. In 1887, schools and refuges were opened in Western Australia as well.

Mary returned to Melbourne in 1889 and found the economy much changed. Factories were closed as depression hit and threw thousands out of work. There were racial conflicts, prostitution, street gangs and criminal activity. Archbishop Carr asked Mary to open a Providence in La Trobe Street (heart of Melbourne).

The strain of the years were catching up on her. She suffered a stroke and for a long time could not walk or talk. In 1894 she visited New Zealand again and with her sisters established a Maori mission and started schools on North and South Islands. They became extremely popular in New Zealand and the sisters returned there in 1897. She set up yet another branch in poor country areas such as Arrowtown near the shores of Wakatipu and Queenstown, South Island. The New Zealand climate suited her, now a woman of fifty-five. 'I am so much stronger that really you would wonder to see how I can climb the hills without puffing,' she wrote to a Sister Annette, her confidante. But the arthritis was so painful in her thumb that she could not keep up with her correspondence.

In 1898 Mother Bernard died and so Mary Mackillop resumed her role as superior general. It is fitting that the order by this time was established in so many places in Australia and New Zealand and now had Mary as their rightful head. This development reflected what was happening in her nation. In 1901 the Federation of Australia was established whereby colonies were united into states under a central government. In 1902 Australia became the second nation in the world to give women the vote. (New Zealand had taken this enlightened step in 1893.)

Mary collapsed in Rotorua, New Zealand, from a stroke leaving her paralysed down her right side. Her mind was unaffected and she had to learn how to write with her left hand.

Just before her death, she advised sisters about how to handle adversity when it confounded them:

Whatever troubles may be before you, accept them cheerfully, remembering Whom you are trying to follow. Do not be afraid. Love one another, bear with one another, and let charity guide you all your life.[10]

In 1909 Mary died and was buried at Gore Hill cemetery in Sydney. When the memorial chapel at the Mother House at Mount Street was built in 1914, her body was transferred to the marble vault there. The memorial slab was the gift from her 'ever loving friend' Joanna Barr-Smith and was inscribed with the simple words:

> *Mother Mary of the Cross [Mackillop].*
> *Foundress of the Congregation of the*
> *Sisters of St Joseph of the Sacred Heart.*
> *Founded in South Australia 1866.*
> *Died in Sydney, August 8th 1909.*
> *Requiescat in Pace.*
> *Amen.*

By the turn of the century Josephite convents, schools and institutions had spread far beyond South Australia. Besides the convents formed under bishops' control in Western Australia, the three country dioceses of New South Wales, as well as Tasmania and Wanganui, New Zealand, there were sisters in the dioceses of Sydney, Armidale, Sandhurst, Melbourne and the South Australian dioceses who looked to the Mother House in Sydney for guidance. Mother Mary's role in holding these distant foundations together entailed an enormous output of correspondence, personal letters to sisters, circular letters to convents, and the ever-present call of official communication.[11]

Throughout most of her life she was plagued with ill health but she wouldn't let up with her travelling to remote areas to contact her sisters, nor with the daily menial tasks in the convents.

Mary Mackillop's life was coloured with cycles of opposition in the face of the enormous popularity of her order. Opposition came from priests and bishops, who it seemed, couldn't cope with a godly woman whom they couldn't control. A woman who achieved her visions in God. Life would have been a lot easier for them if Mary had been both more submissive, more sinful and less persistent in achieving her goals. The Lord had blessed her and her sisters with the extraordinarily rapid expansion of the ministry because she was totally devoted to her Lord and to the poor people in the many communities where she founded branches of the order. The consecration of her life to her Lord attracted people to join the order to in turn serve in humble and demanding ways.

The good news was that despite resistance, God's plan for the education and the meeting of needs of the poor in Australia through Mary and her hardy band, came to fulfilment. This far exceeded anyone's expectations and her opponents' worst nightmares. It's a worthy lesson: in spite of hostilities, God's sovereignty prevailed regardless. (The mark of a godly enterprise is that it is attacked from all sides. If you don't believe me, ask yourself, did Jesus have an easy life? How often was he attacked? Probably as many times as he had dinners.)

Historians tend to polarise figures into either saints or villains but the chain of events, attitudes and behaviour of the main players are usually far more complicated and less extreme in reality, than in the history books. Mary Mackillop would have had her faults like the rest of us, but her many letters to her family, the Josephite sisters and others show a remarkable godly response to whatever life threw at her. Forbearance and adherence to her beliefs and vows of the order were unshakeable.

The more important issue underlying this was the recurring one – under whose authority is the order to operate: to be independent or under the direction of bishops? Did bishops have the authority to re-write the Rule of the order? The quote is also a strong witness to her faith in God to provide for the schools without government assistance. In modern language Mary stood on the word of God as her final authority, and on God's power to provide the finances.

Mary reflected on her busy life and difficulties:

I often feel inclined to envy my quiet country sisters who have the same daily routine and so much peace whilst I am one day in a rough mail coach, again in a steamer in rain and storm, but worse than all, when I have to see Bishops and Priests, and, in the cause of our loved work, have to hold out against all their arguments and threats.[12]

Always a realist, she never denied problems existed. When her rather difficult father died she wrote her mother a sympathetic letter and added realistically: 'I am sure that you cannot regard Papa's death as a trial.'

She had faced the prospect of the worst possible scenario for her beloved sisters when she wrote: 'The Holy work of God has to be attended to and if we are crushed and humbled to the very dust, as also laughing-stocks to all who know us, we must be faithful and look for rest and peace only in heaven.' It is worth noting that girls were drawn in significant numbers to the order knowing full well that their lifework would involve overwork, difficulties, condemnation by the 'respectable classes', at times extreme poverty, etc. They must have been made of stern stuff or wanted to see the Lord as their Jehovah Jireh in their lives. This echoes the same enthusiasm to sign on as the sisters and brothers of the Missionaries of Charity established by Mother Theresa and the thousands of people from various denominations who are drawn, not to comfort, but to working with the poorest of the poor around the world.

We see the Lord sustaining her through many trials and personal losses. She was born the eldest of eight children but only Donald and Annie accompanied her into old age. All the others had died either in infancy or in the intervening years. Her beloved mother Flora drowned at sea when the ship she was travelling on was wrecked.

Accepting suffering as the will of God, and joining it with the Cross on which Jesus Christ suffered and died, had long been part of her life. Now she was more deeply conscious that she was called to share this

Cross. The list of her troubles – the injustices, misunderstandings, and slanders she suffered – is long and
at times hard to believe … her life seemed to have
more than the normal share of the physical pain,
annoyance, disappointment, and disturbance that is
the lot of human beings. Mechtilde later wrote: 'Under
the trials of government, poverty, debt and persecution, she was always uncomplaining, even-tempered
and approachable.' Mary was a sufferer, but not a sad
sufferer… She was always serene.[13]

She knew the Lord in a deep and significant way:
such closeness that only suffering can bring. Mary
must have known the power embodied in the verse:
'My grace is sufficient for you, for My strength is
made perfect in weakness' (2 Cor. 12:9). She shared
a secret with future generations: 'It's love makes
suffering sweet… When storms rage, when perse-
cutions or dangers threaten, I quietly creep into its
deep abyss and securely sheltered there, my soul is
in peace.' What more in life do we want? Mary
Mackillop was 'an extraordinary Australian who
had a vision for a better Australia and followed it
through to the end'.[14]

---

[1] Inserra, p. 41
[2] Quoted in Inserra, p. 21
[3] O'Brien, p. 65
[4] Placid, Sr M., quoted in O'Brien, p. 161
[5] Patricia, Sr M., quoted in O'Brien, p. 161
[6] Letter quoted in Gardiner, p. 83.
[7] Goold, Bishop quoted in Gardiner, p. 106
[8] Mackillop, M., quoted in Gardiner, p. 105
[9] Mackillop, M., quoted in Inserra, p. 31

[10] Written 1909 quoted in Inserra, p. 41
[11] *The Official Mackillop Papal Visit Book 1995*, p. 12
[12] Inserra, p. 33
[13] Gardiner, p. 67
[14] Inserra, pp. 41, 42

Mantle of safety

As a student he was like a strangely-shaped peg, look-ing for the hole into which he was to fit. In time he found the hole and its size was the size of five-sixths of Australia. (Rev. Sir Francis Rolland at the opening of the John Flynn Memorial Church in Alice Springs 5 May 1956)

Outback is an imprecise word: 'remote and usually uninhabited or sparsely inhabited inland areas, especially of Australia, remote from major centres of population'. The vision of the Rev John Flynn (1880–1951) and the Royal Flying Doctor Service, which meets the medical needs of people in outback Australia, is always paired in my mind with my 'big emergency'. While my family and I were camp-ing in a remote spot in country South Australia, I had the worst accident to date: (not much else had happened to me in my first four years of life.) My father recounted the story:

I remember it well. Dreadful! We camped beside a creek midway between Parachilna and Blinman in the Flinders Ranges. You actually fell on the sharp edge of the plough disc barbecue I'd made. God alone protected your eye. Wish I'd known more about praying then. Just outside Blinman was the TB Sanatorium, just a little place with a couple of nurses but they couldn't sew you up. But they mopped you up and told us to try the Flying Doctor Base at Hawker. They radioed ahead for us but he was away until next day. They thought the stitches could wait that long. So we went back to the camp and packed up the next day. We may have driven about 90 km to Hawker. The whole area was ablaze with the wildflowers that had drawn us to the place. It was the South Australian Labour Day weekend in October, a perfect time for wildflowers. You were OK – no complications, but we thought the day's delay may have left a very visible scar. But your beauty is intact.

For the record, on the day, I screamed the place down when the doctor sewed my eyebrow but I received a liquorice all-sort 'for being so good' from the nurse. I clearly remember thinking: 'No I wasn't, I cried all the time!' But I didn't argue I was too well bred.

It is a vast distance from Scotland to the Flinders Ranges in South Australia but in a strange chain of events the two places are linked in the founding of the Australian Inland Mission (AIM) and the Royal Flying Doctor Service. At the turn of the century there was enormous interest about new developments in aviation, radio and medicine. These three came to possess the mind and actions of John Flynn. Born in the town of Moliagul, Victoria, one of the ministry positions he took up was the Presbyterian Smith of Dunesk Mission based at Beltana in the Flinders Ranges.

The Mission stemmed from the generosity of Henrietta Smith. She was given a substantial endowment by her Scottish father, Baron Thomas Erskine (1750–1823), later Britain's Lord Chancellor, when she married Dr Peter Smith in 1812. She became mistress of the manor house Dunesk at Lasswade, near Edinburgh.

In 1839 she bought 162 hectares of land in South Australia, directed that it should be leased for farming and the profit set aside for the Church in Scotland for 'promoting the Gospel in South Australia', including the education and evangelisation of aborigines. (Her son tragically perished while inspecting her land.) In the late 1850s she was told that Aborigines were a dying race so she agreed that the money go instead to the Presbyterian Church in Australia.

Strangely the legacy lay idle, quietly growing for more than thirty years, so by the 1890s the funds had reached the substantial sum of £3000. In 1893 a Presbyterian minister happened to read through some old minutes of meetings and discovered this nest egg. After some more investigations the Presbyterian Church of SA acquired the retrospective rents and income from the estate. In 1894, forty years after Mrs Smith died, the church established the Smith of Dunesk Mission.

Between 1895–99 the Rev Robert Mitchell conducted the Mission in the region 'driving a tilted wagon, with an organ, a daughter who played it and a supply of books.' The Mission in Beltana was on the thousand kilometres railway line from Port Augusta north to Oodnadatta: the sole lifeline for the scattered pastoral communities of the desert area with the coastal towns. To the north of Oodnadatta was Alice Springs (the heart of the continent) a mere eight hundred kilometres away. It is an area where musical aboriginal place names like Lakes Cadibarrawirracanna and Kittakittaooloo and Wattiwarriganna Creek compete with prosaic Lake Conway and William Creek.

Around this time John Flynn entered the Presbyterian Ministry. The year 1910 was a significant turning point for him. Louis Bleriot made history by flying across the English Channel; a triumph that stirred in Flynn a fascination for flying. The future was to see the results. In 1910 he succeeded Revs Mitchell and Rolland in the Mission that then consisted of a run-down boarding house and a nursing outpost. From these headquarters, John made trips to homesteads with horse and buggy, provisions, medicine box, camera, magic lanterns, organ, hymn books and magazines. He distributed books to drovers, miners, railwaymen, police troopers and cattlemen.

Flynn's first ambulance experience occurred in Alice Springs where he heard that there was a critically injured man in the bush. He drove his 'buckboard' to pick him up and brought him back to Alice Springs. He then telegraphed the doctor stationed hundreds of miles away in Oodnadatta, who advised him of appropriate treatment for the patient.

He sowed the seeds for inland communication by writing the 111-page best seller *The Bushman's Companion*. This contained articles on first aid, Bible readings, directions for making a will, hymns, prayers and philosophy. Immensely popular, four thousand copies were distributed through finance from city people. In his *Companion* he wrote what amounted to his calling: 'There are so many gaps in outback life – material, medical, social, religious. Of these gaps, we professed followers of Christ have been all too long neglectful.' The next step was the 'Mailbag League' – city people sent news and letters to those in the outback.

He took the 'call of the inland' seriously. He heard his calling in 1909 when he read the following letter from West Arm, Port Darwin, that, though written about another area in Australia, nonetheless had a lasting impact: confronting him with the needs of isolated communities:

I am eighty miles from a town by land, twenty by sea, three miles from the nearest white woman, two miles from the nearest white man. Chinese and black are my nearest neighbours. There are three churches in Darwin, C. of E. [Church of England], R.C. [Roman Catholic] and Methodist... The Methodist preacher paid four visits to West Arm last year, this year no one will come. The trip by boat costs 7/- return. There are no other ministers in the NT [Northern Territory] – 500,000 square miles of country with 1500 whites, 2000

Chinese and 5000 blacks [Aborigines] living here. Of the whites, fully 500 of the men keep lubras [Aboriginal women] or use them as they want them and nearly all have half caste illegitimate children, whose only future in life is prostitution. There are not 50 Chinese without lubras. There is no law against this evil and there are no missionaries to teach the people right from wrong… what is needed is a mission station close to each of the principal towns, Borroloola, Pine Creek and Palmerston [Darwin]… I know that drink, drugs, and lubras are responsible for nine out of ten hospital cases, and responsible for seven deaths out of ten. Why cannot the Presbyterian Church send up a missionary to the NT, an earnest, enthusiastic married man… give him £100 for living expenses, a certain sum for travelling expenses and let him make his headquarters in Darwin and have regular periods for visiting the outer places of the NT? He would do good if he were a man who put Christ first and who worked for the good of others and spared neither time nor money nor labour in the cause of Christ… Yours faithfully, Jessie Litchfield.[1]

Accounts I read of outback problems which propelled John Flynn into considering the needs of these intrepid inlanders, left me with the question: Why go there anyway? Why didn't people stay in the cities?

At the turn of the century the two million square miles called the Australian Inland was a frightening place. Its few inhabitants were at the mercy of all the extremes of nature and the scattered homesteads were lonely places, cut off from help and news, tiny bulwarks in the huge plains. The greatest enemy of the people was distance – the many hundreds of miles between them and help or companionship.[2]

True as the statement is, I don't want to add to what some non-Australian readers may already think of us, that we truly are 'a weird mob'! I amazed a NZ boy once by casually talking about going bushwalking in Australia. 'With all those poisonous spiders and snakes?' he gasped, eyes as big as saucers. In his estimation of my bravery, I had joined the ranks of the world's explorers – move over Livingstone. Although large stretches of the country are in fact desert, underneath is the Great Artesian Basin covering an area of 1,750,000 sq. km. that supplies water. There were few women at the time of John Flynn because men were not keen to take women into the outback where there were no modern communications or facilities especially for the crucial times when children were born.

I have the greatest admiration for the early pioneering farmers, prospectors and adventurers who set foot in the outback, especially the Top End (top of the Northern Territory, Darwin is the main centre.) The following account of holidays spent about 240 kilometres south of Darwin hopefully conveys the excitement, beauty, isolation and potential terror of the Territory. Unlike the early pioneers, we could return to the civilisation of Darwin after the holiday nor did we have to eke out a living from the land.

I invite readers to 'see' the beautiful spot – Oolloo – from the point of view, not of a family on holiday, but to imagine a family living there permanently. Catch a taste of why people give up cities in preference to the 'back of beyond', and understand the God-given gift of the pioneering spirit. A holiday in the Top End can be either exciting or terrifying, depending on the way we look at it – and the stuff we're made of. The wildlife can attract us or send us running for safety. Territorians take the hazards as just part of living in such a picturesque landscape.

My family's favourite caravanning destination when we lived in Darwin was the Oolloo crossing on the mighty Daly River. In recent times no doubt hordes of tourists have since invaded the place. Not surprising, the spot has much to attract (or scare) them. The spectacular bird life alone; especially noisy, blue kingfishers plunge-diving for fish, would make a lapsed atheist believe in the creation story all over again.

Lurking in the waters were crocodiles. We didn't see any during the day but at sunset we saw, or we thought we saw, well, at least we heard them. We think.

Knowing that there may have been crocodiles both added to and detracted from the holiday. Peering over our shoulders to see if we were being sized up for dinner added excitement to the location. Since we didn't ever see one in the area, in reality there wasn't much threat to losing a child or two.

There was that night though…

On the sandspit at the water's edge we heaped up wood one afternoon for a bonfire that night.

After dark, armed with matches and a torch, my sister and I courageously set off for the sandspit.

A loud rustling in the darkness. We fled back to the van.

'You're back quickly,' my mother said.

'There's a crocodile out there,' we panted.

A crocodile or wild pig, cow, water buffalo, brumby (wild horse) or probably – a child-eating wallaby? On bushwalks she carried a stick to ward off ravaging pigs, or so she teased us kids, but never had to test her pig-conquering abilities. She'd also carry a stick to ward off spiders. Those we did see: big, black with red spots, they made the southern states redbacks look like junior league players (or scarers). They weren't into petty crime like stealing into caravans, to give the occupants heart-failure; they anchored webs to high branches and launched themselves across the dirt roads.

At least they weren't the venomous bird-eating spiders. 'No silly, they don't prey on wedge-tailed eagles – just little birds more their size!' Mmm? They aren't fanciful fiction either. The female of the species is often larger than a mouse. Frogs and lizards can find themselves on the menu as well.

Only a few campers visited our patch of riverbank. Once, we were invaded by a velvety invasion of butterflies – multitudes of species sporting multitudes of colours, sizes, and strange designs. They alighted on the lush canopy over the van.

Thick bush surrounded us; debris in the upper branches reminded us of the ferocity of flooding every wet season. Seeing the Daly in the dry season, it was hard to imagine this calm river breaking its banks and deluging all in its path in the wet season.

We fished for plump barramundi – perhaps fought may be more accurate. My sister snagged a beauty. She was hanging on the line for dear life, thinking she'd end up in the drink for sure, when the line snapped. Her hands were lacerated in the battle.

Fishing on the bank though did at times pay dividends. One holiday we were not alone: a rowdy family disturbed our peaceful nook by their drunken party. Next day, the bleary-eyed father apologised for the ruckus by inviting Dad to go out in his boat to a spot on the Daly where he guaranteed the fish would be biting.

They set out at the right time of early morning, in a boat bearing the latest expensive fishing tackle, used the bait fish would kill for, to the spot where the fat ones just swim around hoping to be caught.

They didn't catch a thing all day.

Meanwhile back at the bank, I was fishing in shallow water. There was no point trying in deeper water, my line was only a few metres long. I'd found it wound around a piece of wood sitting up a tree. Presumably discarded by someone, the makeshift line had been swept away by floodwaters then lodged in the tree, when they receded.

I caught six catfish! Not great eating I grant you, but the triumph was sweet.

There's no accounting for taste amongst some of the river life. We caught freshwater prawns in a bucket submerged in water. The prawns showed an unusual predilection for the bait – soap. One weekend leaving civilisation behind and heading for a simpler lifestyle meant accidentally leaving shampoo behind as well. We had to wash our hair in the river using dishwashing detergent. Mum said the fish would have soapsuds in their eyes. Can fish blink?

We saw the handiwork of a benign resident who picked up the 'size' theme of the Top End. Swimming against the current, Dad and I once crossed the Daly, then laboriously climbed a high steep cliff on the other side. The gouged undercut and exposed tree roots at the top were testament to the surging flow at a less peaceful time of year. Above the flood line was a mound of earth and leaf compost several feet high and many metres in diameter, built by an enterprising scrub fowl to incubate her eggs in.

The wildness of the area accentuates its beauty and forced us to appreciate nature's abundance. Oolloo memories comprise larrikin birds, playing up just for the fun of it, fish wriggling off my line, quiet, clear water and bush that is renewed each wet season but somehow stays the same.

Perhaps crocs have holidays too.

When Jessie Litchfield's letter arrived, Presbyterian Church leaders in Sydney and Melbourne were taking the plight of inlanders seriously. They decided that Flynn should investigate the huge region. He travelled half way around the continent from Beltana to Adelaide, Melbourne, Brisbane, Queensland ports, Darwin and small settlements within a radius of 150 kilometres of Darwin. The NT suffered from poor land, low rainfall, scarcity of labour and the absence of nearby markets.

'Flynn believed that the only way to reach the people of the bush was to share their isolation and loneliness.'[3] He recommended a number of measures to the Presbyterian Church in Australia at its Assembly in Melbourne, on 26 September 1912, in his report *Northern Territory and Central Australia: A Call to the Church*. He included a detailed description of the outback – its geographic, social and economic state.

1. Patrol padres based in Pine Creek (south of Darwin), and in Oodnadatta would visit isolated settlers. Padres would travel by camel, horse and buggy – covering 1800 kilometres of desert on any one journey – and be away for six months at a time.
2. Medical care. He had helped set up the Oodnadatta Hospital and the outstanding work of the nurse there convinced him that other centres could follow the example, starting with Alice Springs.
3. The welfare of the outback people is the responsibility of the whole Australian church and the work should not be left to separate state churches. He proposed a special mission area encompassing the NT, remote regions of SA and WA.

The last thought showed the influence of his childhood moving within the orbit of Catholicism,

Anglicanism and Methodism. (As early as 1940 he was advocating the radical idea of co-operation between Presbyterian, Methodist and Congregational churches in the NT. Australia-wide unity of the three denominations didn't occur until 22 June 1977 with the establishment of the Uniting Church of Australia.)

Flynn told the committee of the anxiety of women bearing children in the bush away from medical aid. This echoed his father's training to respect women and the memory of the death of his own mother at twenty-eight during childbirth. There was no doctor present, no hospital accommodation and no telephone to ring when complications came. He also lost his brother Eugene to TB while he was young. Flynn so admired him that he modelled his own life on Eugene's short one. The deaths and his sister Rosetta's involvement in church affairs caused him to ardently seek the Lord and at only sixteen, he desired to become a minister.

Rosetta assisted him enormously in his efforts. She encouraged donations towards projects through the woman's page column in a local newspaper called the 'threepenny-piece campaign'. John set the schemes and Rosetta did the worrying! She once heard that John had enlisted the aid of a woman in yet another fund-raising project. She wrote:

> Jack's up to some mischief he's wanting you to help him in. Thank goodness it isn't me this time. I'm worried out of my wits with the schemes he gets going.[4]

A lonely childhood without a mother's care, a father who reared him with a sense of chivalry and the loss of his brother in his formative years, had given John Flynn unusual sensitivity. [5]

The response by the church was overwhelmingly enthusiastic. Perhaps they were waiting for a visionary for the centre? They unanimously adopted the report without reservation. Flynn was appointed the superintendent of the new work: the Australian Inland Mission (AIM).

In the space of two years, John Flynn had moved from being a probationer missionary, who had just got through his training by the skin of his teeth, to become the leader of a new mission which encompassed half the continent. He was to hold that position for the next thirty-nine years. [6]

For the first six years with the AIM he set himself three goals:

1. Survey the north and centre to understand the inland.
2. Propaganda: he was an excellent communicator and preached around Australia to garner support.
3. Organise voluntary office teams and support groups in every place he visited for administering funds, etc.

He was not a fiery preacher or orator. Yet it was not clever words that brought responses but stating facts about the conditions in the inland, especially in Flynn's exceedingly popular magazine *The Inlander*, which broke the news of the silent heart of Australia. 'Medicine by Imagination' included a letter sent by a woman in Alice Springs.

> I have a parcel of medicine somewhere between here and Oodnadatta which I ordered on 16 December 1912 [3 months before]. They were for myself and my child who was then about three months old. The latest advice I have about these medicines is that they will not be here for three weeks yet.[7]

Flynn criticised the government about the postal services and other issues but didn't overstep the mark, believing that once they were educated about circumstances then they would change their attitudes. Stories in *The Inlander* exposing deprivations of settlers attracted enormous attention around the nation.

One grateful inlander wrote to Flynn:

> I always feel like giving the AIM a pat on the back because it walked into the Centre ahead of all the others, where Presbyterians were few and far between and with just the thought of doing good, not what extra church people it could get.[8]

Men and women inspired by his compassion for people signed up to join the AIM to serve as nurses or patrol padres or in many other capacities. The passion of his vision backed by statistics, maps and anecdotes from real-life conditions prompted both

Presbyterians and non-church people alike to catch the vision and support with finances and skills. Certainly there were setbacks, difficulties by the score, broken dreams and financial squeezes. During the two world wars finances dropped and some AIM workers signed up for service overseas. Flynn laboured over the text, maps, charts, diagrams and photos for his book *Australia at a Glance* about the geography and economy of the inland. On Christmas Eve 1922 the material was destroyed by fire at the printers. He rewrote it but it did not get into print until September 1924. (No back-up discs in those days!) But God's plan for linking and therefore blessing the isolated townships was a grand vision which could not be thwarted in the long term.

Later on, money came in the form of bequests from grateful women who, as Max Griffiths, author of *The Silent Heart* suspected, 'would have offered to serve in the outback in Flynn's day had they been able. Time and time again, these legacies saved the AIM from financial embarrassment when Flynn and his successors plunged into some new venture with little else except faith.'[9]

Flynn firmly believed that the centre's development was vital for the nation's future prosperity. Wherever there was a project, AIM was there. When the Transcontinental Railway joining east and west was being built, AIM had a welfare tent for construction gangs providing books, magazines, games, letter-writing or a chat with the padre. Volunteers in cities came to church offices to pack huge quantities of literature for the inlanders.

Supporters all over the nation held functions to raise funds, including large affairs in the town halls of capital cities.

AIM founded a number of 'nursing homes' (hospitals) for the sick or injured in the WA, SA, QLD and NT communities of Oodnadatta 1912: Port Hedland 1915, Maranboy 1917, Halls Creek 1918, Beltana 1919, Victoria Downs 1922, Alice Springs and Lake Grace 1926, Innamincka 1928, Esperance 1930, Dunbar 1938 and Fitzroy Crossing 1939. In a roundabout way the earlier aspirations of the benefactor Henrietta Smith to evangelise the Aborigines through the church were realised because the AIM nurses treated whoever was ill or injured, white or aboriginal.

Nurses had to try their hand at every problem. Those at Halls Creek attempted to take the impression for a patient's false teeth. When he received them back from down south he said: 'They fitted like a sentry box. Touched nowhere!'[10]

One of the patrol padres ('Flynn's Mob') enthused that for him life was hard, but good. When not camping around log fires on spiky spinnifex plains, their bed was often on a dirt floor next to brooding hens, or in a truck's cabin. A waterhole became the baptismal font and church services were held in bough sheds, miners' huts or station homesteads. By 1951 this ministry had grown to seven motorised patrols.

In 1922, after ten successful years of growth, Flynn received a rebuke at the General Assembly of the Presbyterian Church. He was criticised for spending too much time on humanitarian assistance and not enough on spiritual ministry. Certainly Flynn was a very practical man. This was reflected during his ministry training. Rather than being an academic, though he had the intelligence, application to his books was the problem. His theological study was 'white-anted' by practical work in his parish. He said the college had to 'let down the slip rails' to let him graduate and be ordained. In response to the above criticism, Flynn said: 'Human responsibility is the ground work of all spiritual success. The AIM is a spiritual agency, working through the medium of a deep sense of human responsibility.'[11]

The next step – taking to the air! The world had been stunned by the breakthroughs in aviation around the war years. For example in 1919 Ross and Keith Smith had won £10,000 prize money by flying solo from Britain to Darwin in 29 days. Bert Hinkler from Bundaberg, QLD in 1928 with *The Times Atlas* for navigation took up the challenge by flying from Croydon in England to Darwin in just 15 days. Sir Charles Kingsford Smith flew from Oakland, California to Brisbane. The affection and hero worship of these aviators was immense, firing the imagination of both British and Australians with the possibilities of aviation in the future. (London's *Daily Herald* predicted that the day would come when test cricket teams would fly between Britain and Australia for matches.)

Clifford Peel from Victoria penned these words as he was travelling towards the battlefields of Europe. Flynn published the letter under the title: 'A Young Australian's Vision – Aeroplanes for the

Inland'. By using those towns, Peel was saying in effect he could see flying doctors servicing 'from West to East, North to South' regardless of state borders.

Extract from his letter to Flynn by Lieut Clifford Peel:

> In the not too distant future, if our church folk only realise the need, I can see a missionary doctor administering to the needs of men and women scattered between Wyndham and Cloncurry, Darwin and Hergott (Marree). If the nation can do so much in the days of war, surely it will do its 'bit' in the coming days of peace – and here is its chance.[12]

Peel made these points:

1. Installation costs of aviation in the outback at that time compared more favourably with costs of building roads or railways.
2. Aircraft flying 165 kilometres per hour would (with refuelling stops) fly from Darwin to Oodnadatta in 12 hours 30 minutes compared with alternative transport that could take 12 days!
3. AIM could station aircraft at Oodnadatta (SA), Cloncurry (QLD) and Katherine (NT) to cover an area of 700,000 sq. km.
4. Four light aircraft cost £10,000. (Peel gave time and distances flown. Today's planes each costs $2 million.)

Peel's letter has gone down in history as the spark for the flying doctor service but he also envisaged planes being used for many purposes such as carrying mail, government personnel, businessmen and household supplies. Flynn reacted by writing: 'Our young friend [Peel], thinks we may do a little stunt of our own accord. Perhaps if he and one of his medical mates want to prove how easy it really is, we will have a fly, just to see!' Now that's the pioneering spirit, pure and simple!

Flynn told Peel to nonetheless keep his eye open for a few likely sky pilots. This bold statement must be put into context: AIM's entire annual budget was about one quarter the cost of the purchase of the planes. But never daunted by trifling matters like not enough money, Flynn was fired by Peel's vision. Although Peel sadly went to be with the Lord during aerial combat over France just 51 days before the end of the Great War in mysterious circumstances, his death did not dampen Flynn's enthusiasm for his vision, but rather strengthened it. This persistence reflects his previous reaction to his brother's death which strengthened his calling to serve humanity.

Flynn worked strenuously with many others to make the vision become a reality. It took them ten years until the Flying Doctor Service came into being in 1928. Ten years was a long time to keep the dream sparking until the rest of the world and technology caught up with it.

Peel's letter prompted Flynn to displace his promotion of railways, with the exception of the Darwin rail link, in favour of aviation. Elsewhere in the world aviation was being considered for civil purposes.

Flynn's persistent writing and public speaking about the outback over ten years began to bear fruit as people, buoyed by the sense of national pride following World War One, felt they could identify with the courage and bravery of inlanders. There was the attitude that in developing the inland at that time they were securing the future of the nation as a whole. Notable people such as the cattle king Sir Sydney Kidman and the press were giving space to the issues of the outback. The Flying Doctor Service and the network of nursing hospitals were described as spreading a 'mantle of safety'. This phrase which has stuck to the history of the RFDS was first used in the title of an interview with John Flynn printed in the Adelaide Advertiser in 1924. The issue was further fuelled by the news of the rescue of a miner suffering from a fractured spine and pelvis from Mt Isa, QLD.

For this mantle to become a reality, Flynn needed the advice of experts in radio, aviators, doctors and the PMG (government communications department). He wrote numerous articles and lectured extensively and gained the backing of industrialists, wealthy graziers, newspaper magnates, E.T. Fiske of Amalgamated Wireless Association, leaders of the British Medical Association and talked with two prime ministers: Hughes and Lyons.

One of his most generous backers was Hugh Victor McKay (1865–1929) who despite little education, became a multi-millionaire industrialist. He and his brothers gained world fame with their invention of the Sunshine Harvester that combined the processes of wheat cropping: stripping, threshing and cleaning grain into one operation. McKay was a fellow Presbyterian to whom Flynn constantly sought advice. He said of his friend: 'The most understanding friend of my dearest dream.'[13]

Surely, that is one of the best tributes any friend could give to another? Unfortunately McKay did not live to see the Flying Doctor Service in operation but he left in his estate £1000 for Flynn and the AIM to experiment the aerial medical service for one year.

QANTAS (Queensland and Northern Territory Aerial Service) was founded in 1920 by Lieutenant Hudson Fysh, DFC, an ex-Australian Flying Corps pilot during the First World War. He was transferred from the Australian Light Horse to fly more than five hundred hours over enemy lines in Palestine. At the end of the war, Hudson with Lieut Paul McGuinness DFC, DCM, helped organise the Darwin to Longreach stage of the historic flight of their colleagues Ross and Keith Smith. Travelling by T-model Ford and horse to prepare airstrips at Darwin, Newcastle Waters and Cloncurry, easily convinced them that the aeroplane was the way to overcome communication problems in the inland.

Sir Hudson remembered their first meeting in 1921 at the Hotel Metropole:

Flynn plunged into a discussion about the possibility of a flying doctor in western QLD. He peppered me

with questions. Where were the most suitable bases?
What were the telephone and telegraph facilities? Did
Qantas have a plane that could carry a stretcher case as
well as a doctor and nurse? ...we did not yet have a
machine to meet all his requirements. In fact, it wasn't
until 1924, when we procured a De Havilland 50, that
we could carry a stretcher case. He was obviously
years ahead of himself, but I felt he had both the ability and the tenacity to achieve his object. We became
firm friends.[14]

With QANTAS' Hudson Fysh and McKay as allies,
Flynn had recruited two of Australia's most respected business magnates of their era.[15]

Fergus McMaster and A.N. Templeton helped
launch QANTAS (registered in Brisbane). 'It would
be difficult to overestimate the value to Flynn's
campaign of Qantas' remarkable record of safety
and service in the outback, and the co-operation of
its principals, notably Hudson Fysh and subsequently, Fergus McMaster.'[16]

Flynn's commendation of QANTAS appeared in
The Inlander in 1921: 'Since the commencement of
preliminary operations by Qantas in 1920 over 1000
passengers have been carried an aggregate of well
over 26,000 miles.'[17]

The QANTAS base in Longreach provided a
BE2A for joy-riding and as an aerial taxi service.
(The original birthplace of QANTAS was Winton
but for practical reasons, the head office was soon
shifted to Longreach.) In 1922 QANTAS won the
contract to fly mail between western QLD railheads
and other centres in the state. Subsidised by the

government, this encouraged rapid expansion of
the company including transporting the occasional
medical case.

In the meantime another hurdle had to be strad-
dled. Huge distances meant poor communications
between settlements. What was needed was a wireless that could connect cattle stations and nursing
outposts with medical bases. For example, the nurses of Hall's Creek and Maranboy Hospital were
hundreds of kilometres from the nearest doctor and
the telegraph line was not reliable. In the wet season the roads were impassable. Nurses often conducted out of necessity, surgical procedures which
doctors normally perform.

Flynn talked about a theoretical wireless almost
a decade before it was introduced. In the twenties
the government was experimenting with wireless
sets at Camooweal on the QLD/NT border. Flynn
spent £57 10 shillings on a short wave wireless set
which he dismantled in order to study. Then he
learned Morse Code. In 1924 he became a member
of the fledgling Wireless Institute of Australia. At
first Flynn did some experiments in radio with
George Towns around the country from 1925
onwards. But the equipment was cumbersome and
too expensive for the average pastoralist to buy.
What was needed was a portable radio that was
within the financial reach of every outback household.

An electrical engineer Alf Traeger from Adelaide
had been experimenting with wireless sets but his
progress was hindered because he needed a ready
supply of portable electricity. He hit on the idea of

using bicycle pedals to generate power. He produced a simple set costing only £33 for making contact with a flying doctor base. In 1929 Alf arrived at Cloncurry with ten new pedal radios and equipment for a mother base. After installation, he went three hundred kilometre to Augusta Downs and made the first transmission on the new 'voice of the inland'. The wireless sets astonished the country people. The immediate and widespread public reaction to the pedal radio revolution, brought generous donations for sets for inlanders.

By 1939, there were more than 150 radio outposts and by 1969 over 1500. It was no longer a medical aid scheme. Transmitting sets were used by drovers to contact their families, for business negotiations and inter-homestead companionship.

Traeger, a Lutheran, believed that God had guided him to invent the pedal radio.

Radios are still precious equipment for people travelling and working in the outback. Tom Bergin and Paddy McHugh retraced the steps of the tragic last century explorers Burke and Wills.

These modern day explorers commented:

Our portable radio was a treasured possession – our insurance policy – for it meant that in the event of a disaster we could get in touch with flying-doctor bases anywhere from Broken Hill to the Gulf of Carpentaria. Not to have taken it would have been irresponsible, for it cost the people of the outback a lot of time and money looking for idiots who ventured unprepared into these parts telling no one where they were going, sometimes paying the ultimate penalty and dying of thirst before they were found. That day we radioed our position to the tiny mission hospital at Birdsville.[18]

In 1928 AIM finalised the historic contract for QANTAS to provide an ambulance aeroplane with pilot and engineer at Cloncurry, flying 38,000 km per year. The Civil Aviation branch of the Department of Defence subsidised mileage and a few large donations helped meet the bulk of other costs. Clifford Peel's dream had come of age.

The first aeroplane was called *Victory*. Fysh remarked: 'How appropriate a name 'Victory' was after the great struggle to establish the service. Imagine *Victory* flying in and landing at some isolated bush homestead to lend aid to some lonely sufferer: 'victory' really meant something.'[19] Arthur Affleck the first pilot used fences and rivers to guide him while station hands cleared trees and anthills (two to three metres high) to make rough runways.

In 1932 Flynn married the AIM General Secretary Jean Baird. 'The man of the silent heart had finally heard a voice which came into his own loneliness and stayed.'[20] What a gorgeous quote!

In 1933 he was awarded the OBE (Order of the British Empire) and in 1940 the Presbyterian College within McGill University, Montreal, Canada, made him an honorary Doctor of Divinity. Between 1939–42 Flynn was the Moderator-General of the Presbyterian Church in Australia.

The Rev John Flynn died in 1951. His ashes were flown to Mt Gillen near Alice Springs and people sent messages of sympathy and praise through the Flying Doctor network from all over the country.

The Royal Flying Doctor Service in 2000 (its 72nd year of operation) employs 45 doctors, 105 nurses and 96 pilots who fly 47 aircraft. And they aren't Tiger Moths! The patron of the Service is Sir James Gobbo AC, Governor of Victoria. In line with Flynn's philosophy, the service is free to patients.

A modern-day flying doctor, Peter Lyall flies out from the mining town of Broken Hill. The service in the region spreads the 'mantle of safety' across 640,000 sq. km. This vast area takes in NSW, SA, and south-west QLD. Peter is part of a team comprising five full-time doctors and two part-time ones. They conduct clinics in remote towns like Hungerford that are too small to sustain either full-time general practitioners or even nurses. They also visit cattle stations to provide bush clinics if needed. Peter is on call for emergencies and available to talk with nurses about cases. Some serious cases are picked up by plane and rushed to country hospitals or to Melbourne. The demand he says varies greatly from times when few calls come through to days when they are very rushed. He said he is enjoying his role because of its variety in fulfilling a vital function, especially for the critical cases.

Coincidental to my writing this piece, the ABC TV showed a programme on the Royal Flying Doctor Service. Peter's experiences aloft were featured in the first episode. A newspaper commented on the programme:

> It was the convergence of technologies that made it all possible. The Gypsy and Tiger Moths were easygoing

planes tolerant of rough airstrips. The pedal wireless, the Internet of its day, was the great liberator from the brutal isolation of the bush. It began School of the Air, let people talk to one another, and also saved lives – it being a law of nature that babies are born in remote places at three in the morning and during a dust storm.[21]

With the opening up of the inland, assisted by AIM and the Flying Doctor Service, Henrietta Smith's desire in the early nineteenth century to evangelise the Aborigines has, in a roundabout way, come to fruition. The spiritual revivals within many remote aboriginal communities today occurred after the opening of the inland. It became a far more attractive place to live once the security of the medical service was operating.

A RFDS story of 2000 concerns an aboriginal baby who couldn't wait for the plane to land. Nurse Kerryn Charman tells the story.

As I prepare for work every morning, I never know what the day will bring… Recently, on a hot outback evening I was tasked for a flight to Hall's Creek, a tiny isolated Aboriginal community in the Kimberley region of Western Australia's far north west, around one hour's flight from the RFDS Base in Derby. A woman from the community was in early labour with her fourth child, and required transfer to the Derby Hospital. When I arrived… the mother-to-be was having occasional, mild contractions. She was terribly excited about the forthcoming birth… I knew it could be hours before the baby's arrival.

We flew towards Derby without incident, but about 45 minutes into the flight the woman, who was still having mild, occasional contractions, suddenly had the urge to push. Labour had progressed rapidly and unexpectedly, and when I examined the woman I could see the baby's head. This little fellow seemed determined to make his entrance into the world almost 26,000 feet above the ground! We had begun our descent into Derby when the action really started to take place, and I knew the birth was only moments away. I had alerted the pilot of the impending birth and asked him to organise a doctor and midwife to be waiting for us when we landed. But as the birth became imminent, I asked him to fly around in a wide circle above the town so that I could deliver the baby prior to, rather than during the landing – the baby wasn't going to wait another minute to see the world. It was a magic moment of my career... This beautiful, chubby, healthy, baby boy was born aboard the RFDS plane over Derby. It was a perfect delivery in all ways – the mum and baby were both fit and healthy and the landing was smooth.[22]

The story of the Rev John Flynn, AIM, and the Aerial Medical Service is exciting not just because of his vision and determination to make those dreams become reality, but because he could encourage countless others to 'see' that the goals were within reach. Particularly remarkable is the fact that most of these influential people (Christian and non-Christian) were city-dwellers who were encouraged to help unknown people thousands of miles away. Certainly Flynn's contribution should be seen in the light of the broader context of the times. Australian successes during the First World War created an improved nationwide confidence and hence willingness to develop the inland to enhance national security.

Aviators were making epic flights, thereby proving the worth of flight for civil purposes. However, Flynn was asking for backing during the upheavals and financial burdens of the depression and two world wars. As I read the history of events I was pleased to see frequently the names of companies which supported the AIM and the service in the early days. These companies are still strong and healthy today and some have operations offshore suggesting the outworking of the biblical sowing and reaping principle.

Flynn was dealt two weighty blows in his early life by the death of his mother and brother. Instead of making him blame God, the experiences propelled him closer to the Lord's heart and hence into his unique calling. Knowing pain and loss, he could identify with the cares and losses of inlanders. Flynn comforted Darwin people by reminding them that God has a special tenderness for men who face the impossible. God knows what Jesus faced.

Flynn's comment is not sexist, remember there were few women in Darwin then. Men were unwilling to bring wives to an isolated and difficult place in the early days. The Flying Doctor Service helped change that attitude. This free medical care allowed men and women to feel secure enough to marry and have children in the outback. Late in life Flynn remarked: 'The joys of parenthood were never to be but maybe I have helped other people to nurture children.'[23]

He thought broadly about ways to service the inland. In so doing he crossed the division between secular and sacred and also denominational and state boundaries. The pastoral care he envisaged concerned meeting spiritual, medical and welfare needs. The nursing outposts, patrol padres, Aerial Medical Service, *The Outback Battler*, *The Inlander*, *The Bushman's Companion*, 'Mailbag League', were all developed with these goals in mind.

He embraced every current technology that could move the goal closer to reality and motivated technical people to drive it. His hobbies, some self-taught, also became essential ingredients in his ministry. Photography, first-aid, lantern slides, writing, were all turned to good purpose in assisting inlanders and to convey to city folk the realities of the bush and inlanders' extensive needs. He was criticised by his denomination because he spent so much time on humanitarian aid rather than spiritual ministry.

In a number of ways AIM indirectly was 'salt' to both country and city communities. Before AIM produced information, the average city person knew very little about the inland, hence the reference 'the silent heart'. *The Inlander* was included as part of the syllabus material of the NSW Education Department. Maps Flynn drew for a 1922 issue were in great demand by the public, as were back copies of all issues of the magazine. People wanting to go to the inland went to the AIM for advice.

Government people travelling in the outback visited AIM hospitals. These places became the foci of community life as regular drop-in centres. Nurses arranged social activities for the townsfolk, especially to welcome or farewell people. They also tutored children, ran Sunday School classes and church services. The AIM policy stated that a nurse must be: 'sympathetic, broad minded. She must be able to enter into the spirit and life of the people, for her advice is greatly appreciated and her example invariably followed. Her presence in the inland is the best possible hope for the future of the church there. She is laying the foundations of Australia's future greatness.'[24]

Prime Minister W.M. Hughes said: 'The AIM is the only truly national work of its kind doing definite things for the development of inland Australia and brightening the lot of the settlers.'[25]

Rev Fred McKay succeeded Flynn in the AIM. He said:

Flynn… was always keen to hear other people's stories about what made them tick. I remember the opening of our first hospital building in Birdsville in 1937… John Flynn had established the original nursing home in 1924 in the old Royal Hotel… in the main street of Birdsville… I thought Flynn as head of the AIM would do the ceremony, but… he said to me: 'You take the chair, Fred. You're the padre here. This is your territory, your job.' That to me was Flynn. He didn't protrude his own importance and was a generous spirit to the extreme, which is why he won the confidence of other denominations and people with all shades of opinion.[26]

In hindsight we see that God had a plan to develop inland Australia. Flynn's idea that populating the Top End was in the national interest proved prophetic. Darwin High School is located on the best real estate in the city, overlooking the harbour near the site of a former meatworks. (Flynn suggested to the government that they build freezing facilities in Darwin.) At lunchtime we used to watch Australian and US fighter pilots zip across the water. The frequent war games highlight our need for defence. We remember that the Japanese bombed Darwin during World War Two and sank a number of ships in the harbour.

The Lord guided the early pioneers to the inland and into a great diversity of industries: mining, cattle breeding and agriculture to name a few. Part and parcel of this development was security and communication for the inlanders. John Flynn was born in Moliagul, the town where one of the world's biggest gold nuggets, the Welcome Stranger was found in 1869. It seems prophetic that Flynn's vision for outback comfort, security and convenience today is worth billions to Australia. This was particularly important when the mining boom exploded in inhospitable areas. He is honoured on the $20 bank note.

God wants to ignite and keep alive this spirit in people – courage to stay with established ministries, and launch new ones. The same persistence and flexibility shown in Flynn's story is vital. God still throws his 'mantle of safety' over difficult times when he assures us: 'Lo, I am with you always, even to the end of the age' (Matt. 28:20).

1. Letter quoted in Griffiths, p. 13
2. Blanch, p. 280
3. Griffiths, p. 20
4. Flynn, p. 50
5. McPheat, p. 29
6. Griffiths, p. 21
7. Griffiths, p. 24
8. Griffiths, p. 36
9. Griffiths, p. 34
10. Griffiths, p. 74
11. Griffiths, p. 62
12. Peel, C., quoted in Griffiths, p. 43
13. Wilson, p. 70
14. McPheat, p. 111
15. Wilson, p. 70
16. McPheat, p. 250
17. Flynn, J., quoted in McPheat, p. 112
18. Rundall, p. 77
19. Wilson, p. 75
20. Griffiths, p. 102
21. Pryor, D., *The Age*, 11 March 2000
22. 'Kerryn's InFlight Delivery', Flying Doctor Service of Australia brochure
23. Wilson, p. 20
24. Griffiths, p. 74
25. Meeting in Sydney Town Hall in 1926, quoted in Griffiths, p. 74
26. Wilson, pp. 33–4

11

My Education for Me?

Have you ever thought about why you received an education? Sounds like a silly question, doesn't it? Reasons vary between people. Did you go to school, then perhaps college, because of parental pressure? Or because you were just naturally bright and university was the next logical step? Or was it to equip you to get the elusive 'good job'? Did you want an education for what you can achieve towards your future goals? What are they?

Samoa was a long way from the sheltered lifestyle that Katrina and Gary Allan and their children, Nicola, Lachlan, Milly and Hamish took pleasure in. They joined Australian Volunteers International who placed them in Samoa for a year where Katrina used her skills as a gastroenterologist. Gary was happy to leave the pressure of corporate life behind and become a house dad instead.

The seed for contributing to the development of a Third World country was planted while Katrina was still a medical student. She worked in Zimbabwe for three months and has always wanted to go back there in the future. Interestingly, she noted that many doctors of her acquaintance had mentioned to her that the highlights of their medical careers had been their terms serving in Third World countries.

Katrina was a little embarrassed when they found out where they were going because she had to ask where Samoa was on the map. Once there, she found it was the perfect posting for her specialist training as the Samoans have a lot of stomach ulcers. The medical staff thought ulcers were caused by acid and treated the patients accordingly but now modern science knows it is caused by infection and that there is a simple cure. Katrina had the rewarding task of teaching the staff how to use an endoscope, a present from the British Government that had not been out of its box for four years. She also made some improvements in public health.

> I really do miss the laughter; we laughed so much at work. Very few doctors in Australia actually save a life in any one day. But over there, kids and adults were coming in who were desperately ill and if I hadn't been there to treat them, they would have died. Sometimes they did die which was very sad.[1]

The members of the family made friends through sport; Gary played soccer and the two eldest boys played for a Samoan cricket team. They also joined a church. The younger two children loved the lifestyle, especially singing, dancing, drinking coconut milk and running around with bare feet.

Gary and Katrina had discussed volunteering frequently, thinking that the right moment when they should go would appear, one day. Then they realised that that day would never come because there were always commitments at home to fulfil.

The issue was propelled in the right direction when she talked with a woman from Australian Volunteers International. Up until then Gary and Katrina's family had lived a fairly typical suburban life before they took the plunge overseas. The children attended private schools and had a comfortable life – swimming pool, etc. After the experience Katrina commented that had they just continued the same way: 'same job, same suburb, same issues... we would never have broken out of the mould. Now we've made some major decisions. We definitely want to work abroad again.'[2]

It is a common experience of people who serve overseas that they return different people, with changed attitudes. Back on Australian soil, the family is involved in several divergent areas of service. Gary now loves teaching canoeing to underprivileged kids, something he hasn't done before. Katrina said:

> I've definitely changed my views on what I want to achieve with the rest of my life. I'm chairperson of the public health committee for gastroenterology in Australia and I now enjoy thinking about health issues that concern the greater population and how we can really benefit the community. I've also volunteered for the Olympics and I'm medical venue manager for the hockey. I've now got more confidence to be able to do these things. I feel like life is so short. I'm already 44 and there's so much more I want to

do... The whole experience has really strengthened the family.[3]

Seeing your efforts in a developing country make an ongoing difference in the lives of those in poor communities, knowing your influence will last long after you return home, sure beats working in an ordinary job in the comfortable West.

Teaching English in a college in China for an academic year was the most rewarding job of my whole working life. Hearing my former students chattering away like natives, knowing they in turn are now teaching students, brought me great fulfilment. Teaching helped China's development by expanding communication and international understanding.

When my Chinese friend in her e-mails pours out her troubles in teaching her university English students, a part of me wants to hop on the next plane and go over.

We hear a lot about people being unfulfilled in their careers in Australia. Chasing self-orientated goals can turn into 'chasing after wind'. Whereas an attitude to serve a needy community would bring a multitude of rewards: most of them unforeseen.

Leaving home for the long-term stint can be daunting (I know!). As Katrina found, there are abundant opportunities to go overseas for just a few weeks or months to have a look at the needs of a country and test if you could play a significant role there in the future. If you decide to stay at home, then you have an opening to financially support those who do go overseas.

I hear you ask, 'But aren't there creepy crawlies in these countries? How would I cope with the down side?' There are creepy crawlies at home too. Yes, I've been through the sickness, homesickness, loneliness, rats and spiders. My mother back home died during my time away. Regardless, it was still an amazing and rewarding experience and I am so glad I took the risk and went to China.

Western colleges and universities provide high academic standards and resources for their students. On Graduation Day perhaps we should consider an alteration to a famous quote: 'Think not what your country can develop for you, but what you can do for a developing country.'

'What is the name of that animal in Australia that has a, er, pocket?' Elly asked. Her friends tried to remember the English word by repeating the Chinese equivalent and mimicked 'hopping' on the spot.

'Koala bear?' one ventured.

I gave them a second to let the name slip off their tongues, but it refused to budge.

'A kangaroo.'

'Yes, yes, that's it,' they chorused.

Opening eyes, opening minds to strange information, being challenged by alternative ways of thinking, living and solving problems – that's what teaching English in China is all about.

This conversation happened at English Corner – not a place but a time. Once a week under trees on my college campus, English Department students discuss every subject known to humanity. An Australian teacher is seen as an asset in these informal affairs. Along with filling in the blanks with the right word, I filled in countless gaps in their general knowledge about countries lying beyond the South China Sea.

'How do you make a telephone call from your hometown to China?'

'What do you do on Christmas Day?'

One lad asked: 'What is the status of women in your country?'

Every day I learned something about the culture, and staff and students volunteered private lessons in Chinese art, dance and language.

Native speakers are important because they teach current usage of words and phrases and correct common errors in pronunciation. English changes rapidly as over-worked clichés are retired and new phrases replace them. But in China, old phrases remain fixed in textbooks and are taught year after year – frozen in time.

'Hello Sam. Long time no see' is as common today in colleges as it was in the West – how many years ago? Students are eager to learn current buzzwords and when to use them, so as to converse more confidently with westerners.

Correcting pronunciation errors is vital to language acquisition. There are sounds in English that are difficult to pronounce. On a visit to a high school I wrote 'usually' on the board.

'What is this word?'

'Ualy,' 40 voices replied (as my students once would have before I came along). I explained in simple terms that without the 's', the word would be incomprehensible to the listener.

Dropping the last sound in a word is also common, making 'halt' become 'hole' and 'mate' become 'may'. My students became so accustomed to ending drills - 't', 'd' and 'k' that when they learned new vocabulary with these endings, they parroted 't', 'd' and 'k' before I asked them to. Emphasising the necessity for the end sound made an enormous difference to their skills. A native speaker could have conversed with them much more easily when they heard the ending to words.

A school principal once chatted to me for hours, obviously proud of his English abilities. He knew what he was saying, but I was baffled from start to finish because he consistently dropped off the end sounds of his words. Unfortunately Chinese teachers who themselves learn errors, teach the errors to their students, who later become teachers, who teach their students... With tact and humility, a foreign teacher can break this cycle and provide needed encouragement to Chinese English teachers who often face limited resources and little ongoing training with native speakers.

Sowing into Third World countries through teaching, not only benefits the local communities but reaps experiences of a lifetime for the adventurous. It is guaranteed they will return changed people and hopefully, their adopted communities will be left with positive perceptions of their nationality.

A couple of China trips were greatly enriched by the antics of two clowns. On stage, or in kindergartens, schools, colleges and universities, they conveyed messages of friendship, forgiveness, acceptance, etc., to children and adults alike. They have this God-given capacity to transform any serious atmosphere they enter, into infectious fun and light-heartedness. A good belly laugh seemed like just what the doctor would order for some of the fearful and stressed people they entertained. Even the most controlled Party member couldn't resist them for long.

At home these same two clowns perform and run workshops at a wide variety of venues for all sorts of audiences. Here's one of their precious stories. They were in the intensive care unit of a children's hospital. Lying unconscious on one of the beds was a little four-year-old girl. Her mother next to her, said that her daughter had been unconscious for a number of days and hadn't responded in any way during that time. A loud boisterous skit was out of the question for the clowns, so instead, one of them gently blew bubbles onto the girl's hand.

Her little fingers moved at the touch of the bubbles. This was the first movement she had made since losing consciousness. Her mother was ecstatic! She knew this was the first step towards recovery.

The clowns originally both came from diverse professional fields and their performances reflect their years of experience and education. God has trained them well for their present callings.

> I'm the doctor who always wanted to be the clown and Jean Paul is the clown who always wanted to be the doctor. Being clown doctors satisfies both our needs.[4]

Dr Peter Spitzer takes medical care for children very seriously. He thinks medicine shouldn't just be about getting the latest equipment but be also about helping children cope with all the stresses of being in hospital. So Peter and his friend Jean Paul Bell, established the Humour Foundation and transformed themselves into Dr Fruitloop and Dr Bubba-Louey respectively. Love the names!

The Humour Foundation came out of their association which started during their university days. Peter was involved in film and modern dance along with his medical studies. After graduation they travelled the world. They talked a lot about how to combine medicine and art and the day came when they had to either 'put up or shut up'. Out of that decision to press on with their dream developed the clown doctors of the Humour Foundation. The Children's Hospital in Randwick, Sydney agreed to take the risk of letting them work there.

Dr Spitzer said that when a child is dying, he or she is still a child and no one is recognising that fact. The child is absorbing the message from others that there is grief and anxiety. The clowns do 'open-heart surgery'. Sometimes they cry and accept that as a natural consequence of the role. They have a specific programme for the specific needs of the child. They ham up medical procedures and use magic and storytelling.

Most importantly each clown leaves something with the child – such as the famous 'red nose transplant' which comes to symbolise something for the child. When the child sees another doctor, she can put the nose on and see the reaction from the doctor. It's fun and empowers the child as well. The smile on a stick can be a comfort while on the way to theatre. They can put the smile on and not be afraid.

The Foundation now has a team of clown doctors for each hospital in which they work. They all wear white coats and stethoscopes but each is a different character.

Peter met the better known clown doctor, American Patch Adams and read his book before starting the Foundation.

> Because of the kind of person I am – I'm a pilot, I have a Harley outside and I'm a world traveller – I guess I'm open to trying different things and the Humour Foundation had a good feeling about it, but most importantly I knew it would be good for the children. The element of giving something back is very strong and for me it shifts my head into a different way of thinking. So as well as helping the children I'm also preventing my own burnout.[5]

Frank and Debbie are the permanent care-givers (similar to foster parents) of a boy, ten and a girl, six both of whom have special needs. The children have lived with them now for some years. They had missed out on some of the treats and mysteries of growing up prior to coming to stay with the parents. When the boy was little, they recalled:

> We'd given him a teddy, which he'd named Morgan...
> We were at a friend's place and when we came out, it
> was dark. He held his teddy up to the sky and said,
> 'Morgan, look at all the lights.' He'd never seen the
> stars before, because he'd always been given his med-
> ication and put to bed very early. He'd missed out on
> a lot of experiences.[6]

Our western society does the same thing in a way. We are continuously bombarded by the launch of new products, many of which want us to believe they get rid of or anaesthetise our problems and give us a greater degree of happiness. In the end we are sedated to the point of not experiencing life in abundance, since that abundance usually involves a degree of pain, discomfort or sheer hard work. Did you ever achieve a high distinction you were really proud of without long hours studying and poring over phrases or maths? Our consumer society encourages us to seek a self-centred, comfortable existence and run away from pain and suffering.

If we retreat from the kinds of mind-expanding experiences that working in a Third World country can provide, then are we like the lad being given medication and put to bed early? We won't see the lights in the sky. We will miss out on so much that is rewarding, stimulating and fulfilling. Jesus spoke of the 'abundant life' not in terms of being sedated from pain but of abundance in the midst of the throes of service for others. No wonder doctors say that the high point of their careers was the term in a Third World country. Yet there are few luxuries there.

In 1896 Albert Schweitzer (1875–1965) at twenty-one years of age realised he couldn't continue to enjoy his comfortable life when others lived in suffering and poverty. He vowed therefore that he would continue tertiary study until he was thirty, to prepare him for his future life devoted entirely to suffering humanity.

It is interesting to note that his university studies, writing efforts and public speaking around the world give the impression to later generations that he was naturally brilliant academically. But his early schooling created much hand wringing by his family because he was dreamy and not very good at his studies at all. For example, as a lad he had to suffer the annual trial in the pastor's study, between Christmas Day and New Year's Day of writing thank-you letters for presents. No brilliant turn of phrase or copperplate handwriting flowed from his pen. The anticipation of this ordeal was enough to reduce him to tears. As an adult, Albert became a generous gift-giver but gifts to nieces, nephews and godchildren carried with them the command never to send a thank-you note to him! He didn't want to repeat the suffering in the next generation.

The difference I believe between his early and later academia is that he had the goal to work towards once he had committed himself to the service of humanity. God honoured his desire and helped him along the way. That drive was absent in his formative years. No one had tried or succeeded in inculcating him with visions of the purpose for his studies. So what was the point of trying? It wasn't until Dr Wehmann started teaching that Albert, impressed with the man, began to concentrate on his studies and improve academically. Wehmann had the gift of encouragement and was well disciplined himself in his own teaching and general behaviour which touched the young Albert.

His music teacher Eugène Münch gave him little encouragement with comments such as this when handing him 'Song Without Words' by Mendelssohn: 'I suppose you'll spoil this like everything else. If a boy has no feeling, I certainly can't give him any.' Albert was hurt because he certainly had feeling but he had been conditioned by traumatic experiences in childhood to protect his emotions carefully. Still, if the comment was giving permission to express his feelings, then express them he would. Münch was much taken aback by the excellence of the musical performance. Albert was accepted.

> The breakthrough was happening on all fronts. In music as in lessons the pent-up talent, once released, soared immediately to undreamed-of heights. At fifteen... he began to have lessons on the big organ at St. Stephen's. At sixteen he was deputizing there for Münch at church services... A puff of wind from the right direction, and the smouldering fire burst out and leaped heavenward with a ferocity redoubled by its long suppression.[7]

There is another theory put forward by James Brabazon:

> The early backwardness of brilliant men [and women] is not uncommon. Perhaps it is simply this, that most of us allow our natural turn of mind, to which we might apply all the energy of a growing creature, to be diverted into the common course of primary schooling – out of respect for our elders and fear of getting into trouble. We are slowed by preformed ideas, our wheels stuck in the ruts. But the interior direction of some men is so demanding that it will not be deflected; and so in the long run they will travel faster.[8]

(So that's what has been wrong with me all these years, perhaps I'm not so dim after all!) Albert came to the conclusion that 'No-one can do anything in defiance of his inner nature.'[9]

The Good Samaritan

A seminary professor devised an experiment when he scheduled his students to preach on the Good Samaritan. On the day he made sure that each student would walk from one classroom to another to preach the sermon. Some students had ten minutes to change rooms, others had to rush not to be late. Each student, individually had to walk down a certain corridor and pass a bum who had been planted there and who was in obvious need of assistance.

The results told a parable. Few stopped to help him, especially those under the tightest pressure of time. When the professor revealed his ploy, the experiment made a huge impact on the class of future spiritual leaders.

Rushing to preach a sermon on the Good Samaritan they had walked past the beggar at the heart of the parable. We must have eyes to see as well as hands to help, or we may never help at all. I think this well-known poem expresses it powerfully:

> *I was hungry and you formed a humanities club to dis-*
> *cuss my hunger.*
> *Thank you.*
> *I was imprisoned and you crept off quietly to your*
> *chapel to pray for my release.*
> *Nice.*
> *I was naked and in your mind you debated the morality*
> *of my appearance.*
> *What good did that do?*
> *I was sick and you knelt and thanked God for your*
> *health.*
> *But I needed you.*
> *I was homeless and you preached to me of the shelter of*
> *the love of God.*
> *I wish you'd taken me home.*
> *I was lonely and you left me alone to pray for me.*
> *Why didn't you stay?*
> *You seem so holy, so close to God; but I'm still very*
> *hungry, lonely, cold, and still in pain.*
> *Does it matter?*
> *(Anon)*[10]

Ken Gire wrote about a child receiving a comment from a teacher. The meaning was far deeper than the words themselves.

The words seem to be saying something besides a teacher's kind commentary on some schoolwork he completed as a child. 'Look over here,' they seem to be saying. 'Look in this window. It is a window into your soul. It is showing you something of who you are, what you love and what you will be doing with your life if you listen to what your life is saying, where it is calling you.'

'The voice we should listen to most as we choose a vocation,' said Frederick Buechner in a graduation address, 'is the voice that we might think we should listen to least, and that is the voice of our own gladness. What can we do that makes us the gladdest, what can we do that leaves us with the strongest sense of sailing true north and of peace, which is much of what gladness is? Is it making things with our hands out of wood or stone or paint or canvas? Or is it making something we hope like truth out of words? Or is it making people laugh or weep in a way that cleanses their spirit? I believe that if it is a thing that makes us truly glad, then it is a good thing and it is our thing and it is the calling voice that we were made to answer with our lives.'[11]

---

[1] '30 Ways to Change your Life', *Sunday Life! Magazine*, 2 January 2000, p. 9

2 '30 Ways', p. 9
3 '30 Ways', p. 9
4 Lasker, p. 12
5 Lasker, p. 12
6 '30 Ways', p. 10
7 Brabazon, pp. 49–50
8 Brabazon, p. 34
9 Schweitzer, A., quoted in Brabazon, p. 34
10 Quoted in Gray, pp. 91–2
11 Gire, pp. 70, 71

12

Let Them See my Father

Years ago while living in Perth, I joined my sister, brother-in-law and two nephews on a holiday in country Western Australia. My brother-in-law was interested in Antarctica where for a time he worked on a building project. So to make the hundreds of kilometres we travelled between mining towns and the picturesque south-west corner of the state less tedious, we listened to a remarkable adventure. My sister had spoken the lifestory of the Irishman Sir Earnest Shackleton (1874–1922) onto audiotape.

With desert or tall timber outside the car, we were transported to icy Antarctica as Shackleton and his band of men explored this forbidding continent in 1907–09 with Manchurian ponies pulling their sledges. The expedition reached as far as 88° 23° south latitude, located the magnetic South Pole and climbed Mount Erebus. (Made us feel cold just hearing the story.)

To recruit men he placed this advertisement in a London newspaper: 'Men wanted for hazardous journey; small wages, bitter cold, long months of complete darkness, constant danger. Safe return doubtful. Honor and recognition in case of success.'

That's realism! A modern-day advertising agency wouldn't approve of the wording. The advertisement hardly painted a rosy picture but thousands wanted to sign up for the expedition. The extreme danger of the venture was the very thing that attracted them. The words of the last line would be all the team would be hanging onto when shivering in the cold and dark. I agree with Loren Cunningham from Youth With a Mission that there are thousands of young people waiting for a challenging, dangerous job that requires them to give up everything.[1]

Wanting a risky life is a gift that is part of being human. God has given it possibly to propel us into the good works that desperately need to happen. The outworking of this gift is seen in varying degrees across populations. Strangely, by God calling us to what seems like risky ministries, he is satisfying that inner need to live life on the edge. Many of us living with everything we need in comfortable circumstances are frequently restless and unsatisfied. Could it be that our need to live life in uncertainty is not being satisfied? In one sense it sounds as though it is against human nature, doesn't it? But we are complex creatures, are we not? God has lots of plans and wants to plunge us into his work and out of our comfort zones. The stories of the people mentioned in this book bear witness to what he can do with lives dedicated to him and to meeting the needs of others. People to whom their creature comforts came second. The results of taking such risks were phenomenal.

Pat Mesiti is a powerful communicator particularly to young people in Australia and overseas. He comments in his book *Wake up and Dream* that there is another undercurrent of thinking today among the young squashing their leadership potential.

> The 1990s have witnessed isolated incidents, such as Nelson Mandela's vision to bring equality to South Africa. But they are still dubbed the Nervous Nineties because this generation is the first to be raised in the Nuclear Age without a potential future. The people of the Hi-tech Age are a people robbed of some of their spontaneity, imagination and individuality. They're also the first generation to face the full exposure of the media. The current generation is seeing widespread moral breakdown. The 'baby boomers' listened to the Beatles and Rolling Stones and watched *The Brady Bunch*. Today's young people listen to Sodom, Sleeping Dead and Madonna and watch *The Simpsons*. With some countries seeing more than one in three marriages end in divorce, the family unit is under attack. Values have become twisted. There is no longer a clear right or wrong. Society wants moral, ethical leaders and dreamers to stand up and point the way ahead. Where are they?[2]

Currently many branches of the western church are experiencing unprecedented wealth. At no time in past centuries has she had so much money, extensive resources, trained leaders to carry through a wide variety of ministries, nor so many opportunities for Christians to gain technical and spiritual training. Why should God adorn her with so much blessing for such a time as this? Is the wealth for her own use – or is it so that she can be a blessing to the nations who have yet to hear the Gospel?

We are blessed by fast and cheap communications through postal and electronic means. Land and air transportation has increased in efficiency in the last few decades. The cost of travel is now within the reach of the average person and within the realms of contemplation for the local church missionary committee.

Advances in technology and linguistics, as well as the multiculturalism of many western nations have opened up the most abundant opportunities ever for learning the languages and cultures of unreached people-groups.

In this technology-prone age, we can instantly gain up-to-date facts and statistics about every country on earth, every people-group, sub-culture and almost every dark corner of the globe which needs to be lit by Jesus' love.

Indonesia, East Timor, West Senegal, Kosovo, Fiji, the Solomon Islands – the images flash onto our TV screens each night. We see the violence, rape, destruction and extreme vulnerability of millions of people and hear their chilling tales of atrocities. But it is easy to filter such information so that our emotions barely receive it. The world at large is so big, so scary we are tempted not to get involved. So our feelings go on standby until the next news item. Perhaps some nights the only blip of reaction the screen elicits, is from the cricket scores or the exchange rates.

Often when we hear sermons about dedication, preachers frequently mention the deeds of some extraordinary missionary or evangelist from some far-flung country we have rarely heard of, nor are we likely to visit unless the Lord decides otherwise. Though there is nothing wrong with those kinds of stirring sermons – we all need to hear them – to encourage and exhort us, there can be something spectacular and therefore remote about them as well.

But when I think of the word 'dedication', so hard to swallow and even harder to live out fully, the concept comes closer to home for me when I think of Mauretta Gould. Her dedication to the welfare and development of her family of four, and in particular, to her little daughter Kristy is truly laudable. Mauretta is a quilter and her story was recorded in an article entitled: 'Mauretta Gould: Quilter and Mother of Distinction' in *Down Under Quilts*: [3]

> Mauretta Gould of Northampton, Western Australia was awarded the 1993 Westpac – YWCA Mother's Award for her dedication and commitment to her role as a mother. The award was presented to Mauretta by Dr Carmen Lawrence at a special ceremony held at the Government Ballroom in Perth on June 10. She was nominated for the award by her sons, Daen (14) and Paul (12) for battling isolation and bureaucratic indifference to give their brain-damaged 10-year-old sister, Kristy, a normal life. Mauretta, her husband Vaun and the three children, live on a farm in the beautiful

Chapman Valley 50 km from the nearest shopping centre. She helps on the farm, looks after their orchard, is gardener, cook and chief carer of Kristy who was born brain-damaged and needs constant attention.

For 18 months Mauretta ran a stimulation program for her, enlisting the aid of three other people and also takes Kristy to Perth 500 km away for her frequent therapy sessions. She fought and won a battle to have her integrated into the local school. The lass was the first severely multiple disabled child to attend a 'normal' school in the district. The mother's ten years of dedication brought rewards: Kristy now walks, attends the local primary school, speaks a few slurred words and rides a bicycle.

Mauretta is a quilter. With all those responsibilities, how does she find the time, I hear you ask? Kristy's reflex problem causes her to sleep for very short periods – perhaps only five minutes. Therefore Mauretta sometimes only has three or four hours of sleep herself, so she quilts… The family home is decked with more than 40 quilts and others have been given away to the helpers in her daughter's exercise program and to the nearby hostel for the elderly. While she sews, Mauretta… keeps Kristy entertained with stories. 'I just constantly talk to her and she might talk to me one day. That would be my biggest thrill,' she said.

Such tenacity. The constant dedication to the young one's development is risky in a sense because there was the real possibility that Kristy may not improve very much. In the face of little day-to-day progress, her dedication to never giving up her goals is commendable and reflects an enormous degree of maternal love. The results can be seen in the lives of other parents of disabled children whom Mauretta has counselled.

Isn't it wonderful to see the respect engendered in her teenage sons to the extent that they nominated their mum for the award?

It is easy when giving honour to people who have struggled yet overcome obstacles and achieved great things, to ascribe innate individual abilities to the person almost as if the person showed unusual super-human abilities while blowing bubbles as a baby in the cot!

But as William Shakespeare reminds us greatness is birthed into the world in several ways: 'Some are born great, some achieve greatness, and some have greatness thrust upon'em.'[4]

Reality is, rather than being extraordinary people from birth, most great people achieve greatness through the problems and circumstances which life presents to them. But most importantly, what makes the difference is the decision they make, and stand by thereafter, to keep pursuing the goals they see are so imperative. From that decision, develops the character that translates into greatness over time. When the world eventually comes to the conclusion that it has greatness in its midst, and decides to honour the person's abilities, it often assumes the virtues were there from birth and magazine journalists prod and poke into the person's past for clues at an early age. But most abilities were developed slowly and painfully through trials, setbacks and victories over many years.

In 1832 a certain man lost his job. Despite this setback he decided to do something most people never even consider: he ran in a parliamentary election. He failed to get the necessary votes. Upon returning to the business world, he failed in business after just one year. He continued persistently to rebuild his business, but two years later tragedy struck – his sweetheart died. The following year, 1836, the pressure caused him to suffer a nervous breakdown. This man had two options: to give up and accept that he was no good, or to keep on. He chose the latter. Despite the breakdown, business failure and personal tragedy he continued to have great political aspirations. In 1838 he ran in another election, for the role of parliamentary Speaker. He lost. Five years later he campaigned for the American Congress. He didn't have the numbers. In 1846 he again ran for Congress, and this time he succeeded – fourteen years after making his first attempt. Victory, however, was short lived, for two years later he was defeated again. In 1849 he campaigned to return to Congress, but lost. How many people would have kept on going? This persistent dreamer did. Despite suffering the humiliation of more than twenty years of failure, five years later he launched another campaign – this time for a seat in the US Senate. He was defeated. In 1856 he put his name down to become the next Vice-President of the United States. He lost. Again, in 1858, he campaigned to join the Senate. Again he was defeated. Just two years later, this man with a huge dream that he never let go of was named the sixteenth President of the most powerful nation on earth. He was Abraham Lincoln, possibly the greatest leader the United States ever had.[5]

Being a dreamer and running with the dream often means running the course solo and meeting brick walls of indifference – or so it seems.

A few years ago I was on my usual round of recruiting for the next mission and getting very weary and jaded by the indifference of the countless numbers of people I asked. They were not concerned about the needs of others beyond their immediate circle of family, friends, and church. For comfort, I reminded myself that over the years the Lord had sent a remarkable number of dancers to me – out of a country that has very few dancers and even fewer trained ones sitting in pews. To say to someone 'Come to China!' is a big suggestion, considering the thousands of dollars needed to do so. To say 'Come to China and dance!' is an enormous request, but some miraculously responded. (And even more miraculously produced the money.)

Nonetheless, out of the total number I approached seeking a variety of support; dancers, finance, prayer, etc., the number who responded in one of these ways was very small.

Bitterly disappointed and feeling very alone in the whole ministry, it was difficult not to get resentful year after year. It was difficult also to think through the issue objectively. Was I just getting too pushy? Should I just go home, pray and wait for people to come to me instead?

For years I had been smiling sweetly at people as they – also smiling sweetly – said that they would not come with me on the tour. No, they were not interested in coming to our fund-raising functions nor helping us with donations nor prayers nor in

even being interested in continuing this conversation... The hardest part was not that it was a slap in
the face for me and the team, but while speaking, I
could vividly see the faces of the kids in the villages, the college students struggling with their
English classes, the government officials burdened
by toeing the line. All wanting to find purpose and
meaning for their lives.

I never knew when to challenge and feared putting my foot in it well and truly and hence cut off
any potential support that I might have gleaned.
And if I did challenge, what would I say anyway?
Where is my biblical or other basis to confront them
about their lifestyles and priorities of time, money
and energy? Am I the one to confront or should
God or someone else confront them? For all I knew
they could have been giving until it hurt to 50 other
organisations anyway. Were those who didn't
respond sinless before God for refusing such an
opportunity for caring?

But when I read my Bible I saw that the great
commission was clear: it couldn't have been written any simpler. Shouldn't they feel compassion
and at least prayerfully consider this option and
talk it through with me? Isn't the picture painted
by the Bible one of a church where there is a constant movement of people and resources to and
from the mission field? While some are going away
or resting after their time in ministry, others are
training to go at some point in the next year or so.
Still others are giving their prayers and finances
sacrificially to enable members to be fruitful in
their callings. That was the exciting ideal that

seemed so reasonable to me. Why can't others see this simple model?

In the middle of my muddle, the Lord stepped in and cut through my abstract thoughts with one terse comment from Hudson Taylor. While standing at a bus stop on a street, I read a quote from a book. (The quote hit me so hard, I found myself breathing deeply like an asthmatic and had to recover my composure before the surrounding pedestrians gazed dubiously at me.) His pleas to readers settled the question for me once and for all.

In 1865 Hudson Taylor, the remarkable pioneer of the modern missionary movement, constantly spoke about the 380 million people in China:

> Do you believe that each unit of these millions has an immortal soul? And that there is none other name under heaven whereby they must be saved? It will not do to say that you have no special call to go to China. With these facts before you and the command of the Lord Jesus to go, you need rather to ascertain whether you have a special call to stay home.

To go, or to stay home and support others to go, these are the options.

The yearning for the 'good life' and bowing down to the pleasure principle as the guiding light for everyday motivation comes packaged with a warning. Western society insulates itself from as much pain and discomfort as possible. As Tim Costello in his book *Streets of Hope* reminds us, every advertising agency looks for the best way to make their client's product sell via the 'comfort appetite' of the public. If the product can be smelled, eaten, touched or can usher in hassle-free days, then it is sure to be a winner in the marketplace.

In the absence of pain people lose a degree of their ability to later feel pleasure as sharply as nature intended they should.[6] The past presence of one aspect heightens the sensation of the opposite. Has our pleasure-orientated society made itself anaesthetised against pain, or at least less sensitive to suffering humanity?

If God wants us to grow up and become sensitised, he will do whatever he can to bring about that consciousness in us. He may begin to rattle and shake the 'pleasure principle' our society and economy rests on. The resultant pain and discomfort will trigger a greater awareness of the suffering of brothers and sisters elsewhere and lead onto a new or deepening ministry.

If this happens, the pain of loss, frustration and disorientation should reap a harvest in us of greater prayerfulness and action. There is nothing like a mishap or denial of access to the 'pleasure principle' to bring about enhanced maturity and godly character in growing, open Christians. All it takes is prayer that God will show us what is the lesson to be learned from the circumstances. Yes, we kick and scream, don't we? Well OK, I do.

This sounds as if God deliberately brings bad things into our lives in order to teach us a lesson: 'He must be good, he's suffering so much!' This is not what I am saying. There is evil in the world brought by the enemy. But whatever the situation the devil meant for evil, God can turn around for our good. He can develop godly character, which bears fruit later on, in those who are submitted to his teaching.

To those wanting to minister to particular groups of people, God speaks to them when they themselves are going through testing times. They are led to see their own limited suffering as analogous to the suffering of others in the group. Opening the window of understanding in this way brings with it a God-inspired depth of compassion and increased tenacity to the ideals of the ministry. Those who have learned the lesson well, eventually live and breathe the ministry. Their passion is a reflection of God's passion towards those he wants to bless.

In order for us to have a vision for a ministry, we must see with the Lord's eyes of compassion first. He shows us the needs-within-needs within a situation.

> *After these things the Lord appointed seventy others also, and sent them two by two before His face into every city and place where He Himself was about to go. Then He said to them, 'The harvest truly is great, but the labourers are few; therefore pray the Lord of the harvest to send out labourers into His harvest.'*
> *(Lk. 10:1–2)*

Gloria Kempton talks about the loneliness felt by some who decide to passionately love their world.

Sometimes when we move closer to the [passionate] edge, we encounter loneliness. We are growing older and wiser, and it makes sense that we should have more of the answers of life. Yet we seem to have more questions and fewer answers than ever before... we look at everyone else, and they seem to be moving merrily along in their lives... getting their act together... We feel we're standing still and everyone is moving ahead... The closer Jesus drew to His crucifixion the less He was able to 'win friends and influence people'. There weren't many folks crowded around His cross. Even His good friend Peter denied he knew Him.[7]

Any place the Lord is calling us to is in his own plans to visit. So we wouldn't be the first people on earth to visit the area: although before travelling there and during the times of opposition and testing, before the fruits appear, it certainly may feel as though the Lord didn't have any plans to drop in for a pastoral visit. It may indeed feel as though he just sent us out, cap in hand and waved goodbye from the doorstep, without a promise of going there too. But this sense of abandonment is a lie from the devourer who knows that discouragement is our strongest adversary. At these times we must remember that after the giving of the Great Commission, He also promised 'and lo, I am with you always, even to the end of the age' (Mt. 28:20b).

Restlessness is a common part of the process of ministry. It does not necessarily mean that there is something wrong spiritually. It may mean that God is moving a little apart so that we must reach out to him further and stronger in ways not done when things were going along without the restlessness.

Gloria asks us to seek out ways to see situations as opportunities for expressing this love. Ephesians 5:16 urges us to make 'the most of every opportunity, because the days are evil' (NIV). Other versions translate this passage 'redeeming the time'.

> It's developing the mental attitude that says, "How can I creatively seize this moment and make it matter? What is this moment offering me?"…If you're in the process of developing a creative personality, you won't have to wonder how this happens and you won't have to try to make anything happen. Creative seizing of the day will happen because your eyes are finally open and you're seeing the day. Those moments were always there for you to grab – you never saw them before, let alone thought about grabbing them and making them yours.[8]

Pat Mesiti speaks of an occasion when Mother Theresa seized the day to everyone's amazement:

> One of my favourite illustrations of [Mother Theresa's] courage and single minded attitude happened after she had spoken to the United Nations in New York. She decided to visit a maximum security prison not far away and ended up speaking to four inmates with AIDS… Mother Theresa was spurred into action. It was the Monday before Christmas, but all the same she went straight to the Mayor of New York and asked him to contact the governor, Mario Cuomo.

'Governor,' she said over the phone, 'I'm just back from Sing Sing and four prisoners there have AIDS. I'd like to open up an AIDS centre. Would you mind releasing those four prisoners to me? I'd like them to be the first four in the AIDS centre.'

'We have 43 cases of AIDS in the state prison system,' replied Cuomo. 'I'll release all 43 to you.'

'I'd like to start with just four. Now let me tell you about the building I have in mind. Would you like to pay for it?'

The governor was bowled over by her intensity and agreed. Mother Theresa then turned to the Mayor and stated, 'Today is Monday. I'd like to open this on Wednesday. We're going to need some permits cleared. Could you please arrange those?' What fierce determination![9]

I was once told that one of the marks of a God-inspired ministry is that long after the founding visionary of the ministry has been called onto a new path, that the ministry still continues to flourish and grow. Judging the comment against the history of my dance group and other ministries I have seen, I think there may be some truth to it. The endeavours of the people mentioned in previous chapters also bear witness to that.

'One Solitary Life' (Anon)[10]

He was born in an obscure village, the child of a peasant woman. He grew up in still another village, where he worked in a carpenter shop until he was thirty. Then for three years he was an itinerant preacher.

He never wrote a book.

He never held an office.

He never had a family or owned a house.

He didn't go to college.

He never travelled 200 miles from the place where he was born. He did none of these things one usually associates with greatness.

He had no credentials but himself.

He was only 33 when public opinion turned against him. His friends ran away. He was turned over to his enemies and went through the mockery of a trial. He was nailed to a cross between two thieves.

When he was dying, his executioners gambled for his clothing, the only property he had on earth. When he was dead, he was laid in a borrowed grave through the pity of a friend.

Nineteen centuries have come and gone, and today he is the central figure of the human race, the leader of mankind's progress.

All the armies that ever marched, all the navies that ever sailed, all the parliaments that ever sat, all the kings that ever reigned, put together, have not affected the life of man on earth as much as that

One Solitary Life

[1] Cunningham and Rogers, p. 59
[2] Mesiti, p. 185
[3] 'Mauretta Gould: Quilter and Mother of Distinction',
    Down Under Quilts Vol. 6 No. 3 (1993) p. 14
[4] Shakespeare, W., Twelfth Night, act 2, scene 5
[5] Mesiti, pp. 148–50
[6] Yancey (1990)
[7] Kempton, pp. 61–2
[8] Kempton, p. 144
[9] Mesiti, p. 183
[10] Quoted in Gray, p. 262

13

Trembles When we Pray

The one concern of the devil is to keep the saints from prayer. He fears nothing from a prayerless work and prayerless religion. He laughs at our toil, mocks at our wisdom but trembles when we pray. (Samuel Chadwick)

The Market

The flies buzzed around us as we walked through the market across the road from the college. A trickle of perspiration was mopped by dust blown onto my face from the dirt road. 'Market' sounded a fine title for this collection of a dozen or so street vendors. On either side of the narrow lane, farmers from outside town had laid out their fruit and vegetables on ancient sacking and squatted behind them, hoping they would go home with a good day's takings. Shoppers regularly scattered to the outer edges of the pieces of sacking, next to the sellers, when trucks forced their way through. Clouds of smoke blew out of the exhaust pipes as they slowly moved within inches of bunches of shallots

and baskets of eggs. The sturdy trucks lumbered by
so frequently I wondered if there was a construction
site further along the lane. Why choose the market
lane to drive down, of all roads?

I was with Ramona, a fellow teacher from the
college who wanted to interpret, choose the produce, bargain for it and generally do everything for
me, as we bought my fresh supplies. I was molly-
coddled and bossed around in the same breath. This
was my first excursion to the market since I arrived
a few days before. She was also keen to teach me
from day one how the social system worked and
my place in it.

At last I found the potatoes I was searching for. I
squatted down to take a closer look at them and
smiled at the tired and weather-beaten woman
squatting behind her vegetables. My chummy companion snapped out of me any such silly notions of
friendliness, by violently whacking me on the arm.

'Get up. Don't sit down in front of them!' she
barked.

I jumped up to stop myself keeling over from
the impact. She launched into an important lesson
about how I must show my inherent superiority
by standing above and bending over the produce
– and hence 'down' on the 'peasants'. It was wrong
to express any feelings of equality and also dangerous because they may take the advantage and cheat
me.

Tirade over, potatoes bought, foreign 'student'
suitably tamed, she turned on her heel and walked
off, expecting me to pad after her. Smarting from
the object lesson, the word 'cheat' rang hollow in

my ears because I was already paying so little for the food. A bunch of shallots or a handful of water chestnuts were so inexpensive; they would barely scrape within the equivalent range of the value of the Australian dollar. I could have paid double for everything I bought without denting my salary very much at all. Certainly I was happy to do a little to give these people a better income.

Months later Ramona proudly told me that she was the first member of her family to go to university and, in the same breath, that she came from 'peasant' stock. Did she want to blot out any reminders of her family's past? Did she not want to get too close?

I hoped this was the first and last shopping spree with Ramona. Heaven heard my plea and agreed. Anyway, I had a much more necessary lesson to learn about this forlorn, abrasive place.

Shopping excursions once or twice a week afterwards were a lot more fun because a student or two or an even larger knot of chattering girls accompanied me.

They diligently interpreted, haggled and did their best at escorting me. One day after the first shopping spree, I separated for a few moments from my companions after spying some carrots a few feet away. I squatted in front of the neat pile and looked into the face of their owner. A heavy weight fell on me as I looked at the man. His face, features and appearance were no different to all the other vendors sitting jammed with their backs against the buildings, bordering the lane.

Now, at close range and with a smile to the man, God opened a window to see what he saw from heaven.

An old pair of filthy trousers, badly frayed where hems used to be, were held up by a scratchy piece of twine at the waist. A once-white shirt hung lifeless over a skinny body under a blue-grey jacket.

Most of the seams on the man's apparel were giving up their effort to keep the garments together. Holes and runs of threads told a story of hard work with few returns in material wealth and inward prosperity. The abundant life had never touched this man's household in his short life. His eyes said it all – through his shy, slow smile I saw grinding fatigue, hopelessness and despair and a host of other emotions jumbled together, exuded from him.

As he painstakingly sorted through some soggy, torn notes of low denomination for my change, I felt frustrated we couldn't communicate. I didn't know his dialect. Culturally we were continents apart. My clothes were embarrassingly too bright. I wanted to give him some word of encouragement or help him along the path to material prosperity: to show him God knew and God cared.

I could buy a few carrots from him.

And I could pray.

I could bring before the throne of grace every imagined picture of prosperity for his mind, body and spirit and for his family. Such imaginings could soar above the pessimism engendered by the experience. I didn't have to pray for inspiration about what was the 'key' or specific prayer point for this man. I realised how limiting that version of theology was. An overwhelming sense of the common humanity for all people groups flooded my mind: what I wanted for my family and friends was the same as what I wanted for him. We may be a continent away in language and culture, but the needs and desires were the same.

I wanted so many blessings to flow into his life, but still, how limited my thinking was and how stingy my prayer list compared to the vast list of blessings the Lord wanted to be fulfilled in his life! It is sobering to realise the infinite scope of God's knowledge about the man: God's unfathomable omniscience. Even his wife or best friend know him only as an acquaintance in comparison to the depth of understanding God has of him. I hoped my prayers reflected that depth and breadth.

God woos us to see through his eyes the bigger picture, to pray for it and propels us to action to alleviate the problems around us in the community or overseas. Paul Borthwick encourages us to pray with a world-wide focus:

> Feeding our vision for the world through current events means that we are interested in what is happening in the Middle East, that we respond in prayer when a typhoon hits Thailand, that we intercede on behalf of black and white Christians in South Africa, or that we seek to understand the dynamics of rich-versus-poor and capitalist-versus-communist struggles that occur in our world.[1]

He asks us to use prayers of all lengths:

> Our prayer in response to worldwide knowledge
> may mean active, consistent intercession for one
> particular geographic location or one people. It
> may also mean the lofting of 'prayer arrows' in
> response to needs we hear about. A typhoon, earth-
> quake, terrorist attack or revolution may not be the
> topic of my daily prayers, but there is no reason not to
> respond by a single prayer at the moment I hear about
> a need... The one-time 'prayer arrow' directed
> upward to our heavenly Father serves to remind us of
> who is in charge.[2]

Creative ideas come into our brains, to displace the
negative ones the devil would have us concentrate
on: 'How do you think that will ever work?' 'You
can't do anything anyway, the problem is too big' or
the grand-daddy of all lies: 'Who are you anyway?'

Deciding to become fully aware, open, sensitised to things we see and hear, to be motivated to
the point of prayer may leave us vulnerable and
defenceless to be 'eaten up alive from the inside
out'. The pain of the emotional experience pound-
ing on our hearts time and time again may seem
too much. We want to hide behind leather blinkers
and reinforced steel breastplate. It's all too overwhelming.

Is there an antidote?

By seeing the bad in all its fury, we become much
more sensitised to experience more fully the good
around us. We can more willingly thank God for
one's stable family, friends and community, rejoice

over the last round of answered prayers and miracles in the suburbs or whatever it is that is worthy in our part of the world.

Secondly, whether we realise it or not, bit by bit God is strengthening us. Paradoxically, along with the sensitivity comes an inner toughness that stands us in good stead if God asks us to act sacrificially in the difficult situation. The Lord can bring about a softening of heart and personality in order for us to see and feel a situation as he does. Then over time he brings a toughening of resolve and spirit in order to use us to get the situation changed through perseverance in prayer and effort. No one can deny the godly toughness of Mother Theresa (despite her diminutive stature). The same could be said of her own sisters and thousands of others ministering on the mission field today.

> *Therefore we do not lose heart. Even though our outward man is perishing, yet the inward man is being renewed day by day. (2 Cor. 4:16)*

Here is the promise we must appropriate when we feel emotionally drained.

Paul encourages the Corinthians with a word about this inner toughening process:

> *We are hard pressed on every side, yet not crushed; we are perplexed, but not in despair; persecuted, but not forsaken; struck down, but not destroyed – always carrying about in the body the dying of the Lord Jesus, that the life of Jesus also may be manifested in our body. (2 Cor. 4:8–9)*

We are not rendered a paralytic even though our emotions may threaten otherwise. The Lord's strength is available to direct us to continue to pray and act as the Holy Spirit guides. Someone who runs away from frightening evil circumstances and does not want to fight in the prayer realm, can appear to be tough and callous, uncaring. Perhaps he or she is soft on the inside and cannot handle the situation, it's just too dreadful. God changes us so that we are tough on the inside and soft on the out-side and hence sensitive to others' pain and situa-tions.

It must be the experience of all Christian workers in a Third World country. Surely, the day arrives sooner or later when everything inside you cries out: 'Lord, this is too much, I'm just not strong enough. I don't have the right personality. You made a mistake picking me, get someone who's tough.' I'd heard too many stories of crime and injustice, passed too many poor people on the street, too many frail elderly, disabled beggars, ragged children...

'That's why I picked you – because you are soft.' Early in my stay these words reassured me that the Lord knew exactly what he was doing. I drew enor-mous strength knowing all the 'soft bits' in me were not only fine by God Almighty, but in fact what he wanted for the ministry.[3] Pain of all sorts is to draw our attention to something. If God wants to draw us to see something in the media, then we need to take notice of the pain it may evoke.

Philip Yancey, in his book *Where is God When it Hurts?* mentions the work of Dr Paul Brand concerning pain. Dr Brand declares: 'Thank God for inventing pain! I don't think he could have done a better job. It's beautiful.'

> We dare not shut off the warning system without first listening to the warning. A tragic example of someone not heeding the warning occurred in a NBA basketball game in which a start player, Bob Gross, wanted to play despite a badly injured ankle. Knowing that Gross was needed for the important game, the team doctor injected Marcaine, a strong painkiller, into three different places of his foot. Gross did start the game, but after a few minutes, as he was battling for a rebound, a loud snap! could be heard through the arena. Gross, oblivious, ran up and down the court two times, then crumpled to the floor. Although he felt no pain, a bone had broken in his ankle. By overriding pain's warning system with the anaesthetic, the doctor caused permanent damage to Gross' foot and ended his basketball career.[4]

God sends the good often just when we are overwhelmed by the evil we see, to assure us of his intrusion in the workings of the enemy.

Go Forward

> Rest in Me, quiet in My Love, strong in My Power. Think what it is to possess a Power greater than any earthly force. A sway greater, and more far-reaching, than that of any earthly king. No invention, no elec-

tricity, no magnetism, no gold, could achieve one mil-
lionth part of all that you can achieve by the Power of
My Spirit. Just think for one moment all that means.
Go forward. You are only beginning the new Life
together. Joy, joy, joy.[5]

John Perry wrote a song about the work of Jackie
Pullinger and her team of dedicated disciples in
Hong Kong called 'Let Me Show You' based on
Isaiah 58:6–9.[6]

> *Out across the South China sea is a land that's*
> *drenched in mystery*
> *Where people live to die by day and hope the dragon*
> *takes the pain away*
> *Where the ancient and the modern meet*
> *Where the water almost hits the street*
> *So many people with so much need*
> *It's busy business when there's mouths to feed.*
>
> *Let me show you what love can do*
> *Let me show you what love can do*
>
> *To the city that keeps growing higher comes the power*
> *of the sweet Messiah*
> *Reaching out with hands of love to heal, to help to feed,*
> *to share, to cry, to feel*
> *I've seen the needle and the damage done*
> *I've seen the glory of the Risen Son*
> *I know the two can never live together*
> *I know the Son of God will reign forever.*

Let me show you…

Picture a place where you can make your bed
When you're homeless and you're on the street
Picture a place where you can lay your head
A meal and a smile and somewhere to rest your feet
Beat the street, beat the street.

And we who live in our suburban ease ignore our
brother begging on his knees
Our ears deaf to his silent pleas, our eyes blinded by
our luxuries.

Let me show you…

Jackie Pullinger left her familiar surroundings in Britain and caught a ship – not knowing which port she would get off at. Hong Kong became her destination. For over thirty years she has been working among the poor and destitute, prostitutes and Triad gangs. Rehabilitating opium and heroin addicts the 'Jesus way' became her calling.

Whenever I am mulling over the frustrations of unanswered prayer particularly to do with missions, I constantly come back to the challenge of Jackie's experience of the power unleashed by speaking in tongues. Is it any wonder, God appreciating our limitations of perspective, that he gave us the gift of tongues: when our English (French, Indonesian, Swahili or whatever is our mother tongue) fails to convey what our hearts and minds struggle to communicate?

She comments on her own frustrations in the beginning when she tried to reach people for Jesus.

Looking back now, I can see how ridiculous it was to be walking down alleyways talking intensely of Jesus. Of course, no one could respond to words about Christ. They had never met him and had no evidence of his love. When I checked, I found he had never done it that way either; instead of declaring 'I love you', Jesus had shown his love through action. He opened the eyes of the blind man, caused the lame to leap for joy and fed 5000 hungry people full to bursting. There seemed to be a vast credibility gap between the Christ I was preaching and what I was doing. This was shown in graphic parody when I went with two friends into a Walled City street where over a hundred men were sprawled chasing the dragon (inhaling heroin through a tube held over heated tin-foil)... we smilingly gave out tracts which spoke of the love of God and salvation through Jesus. There was even an address where any addict who could read it, and who was alert enough to remember the time, could find out more by attending meetings. Most threw the paper into the sewer but the canny carefully rolled them up and used them as spills and funnels to inhale the dragon fumes. It was so frustrating to read of a man who healed all who ever came to him – who promised his followers would do the same – and yet to be handing out a paper substitute. I wanted to do it like Christ did it. I wanted to learn how to heal the sick and see miracles. If this did not happen the gap would widen into a chasm.[7]

Jackie organised a youth club and ran camps, out-ings and other activities that the Triads and their girls loved attending but frustratingly, she did not see them change in any way. They still fought, lived off prostitutes and protection money and sometimes killed. Then the Lord introduced her to the secret behind the miracles we read about in the scriptures. She gained the gift of speaking in tongues.

> I spoke in tongues when a young Chinese couple prayed that I would receive power to make Jesus real to others. It was not emotional for me... Now that I experienced the same as Jesus' disciples, I expected to rush into drug dens, lay my hands on all the emaciat-ed ruins and see them leap up healed... Then I learned that praying in tongues was to help people when they did not know how to pray or had run out of words. Desperate by this time to see evidence of God's power in action I began to pray privately in tongues for the dying in the Walled City.

Extraordinary things began to happen after six weeks. She wondered if perhaps her Chinese had improved remarkably.

> A gangster fell to his knees in the streets, acknowledg-ing Jesus and weeping. Another, who had been badly beaten up, was miraculously healed. A young boy just initiated into the Triads left the 14K and others gave up their organised businesses. Praying in tongues was making me more sensitive to what the Holy Spirit was doing. Soon I lost count of the number of changed lives around me.[8]

There are countless stories originating from the
ministry of Jackie and the work of others at Hang
Fook Camp. I'd like to share some of my favourites
from her book *Crack in the Wall*.[9]

Goko, the Triad leader had seen the 'power of the
heart' and many of his sai lo's left the Walled City
to start new lives. So the story goes, he sent a message to another leader on Hong Kong Island asking
for gang members to help fight in Kowloon City.

'Sure, but what's happened to your own men?'
came the reply.

'Well,' replied Goko, 'half of them are drug
addicts and the other half are Christians, and they
all make lousy fighters.' That's the evidence of
being the salt of the earth and changing the community around.

But eventually he turned to Jackie for help with
his unruly sons. He thought the church would do
them good.

Jackie was blunt. 'No, they'd hate living in my
house. They don't believe in Jesus, and you can't
force them to. It's your fault they're becoming like
they are – they're following your example. Why
don't you follow Jesus – it's about time?'

'I can't not believe in Jesus,' he said, 'I've seen
too much to deny that. But I can't follow him
myself. You see I use illegal and threatening meth-
ods to collect money, and I couldn't do that if I were
a Christian. If I'm going to be one, I'll be a real one.
Now if God could guarantee me $20,000 a month
that would be different.'

It was going to take being caught for criminal
activities to make Goko think again. A few months

later he was remanded in custody awaiting trial for possession of a large quantity of opium. An addict himself, Jackie told him to pray before the pains he would go through during withdrawal, started.

She heard him sentenced to three and a half years in prison. In the five minutes Jackie was allowed with Goko afterwards, she saw a broken man weeping and saying he wanted to change. After his heart-commitment to follow Jesus, he started speaking in tongues and prophesying. Their 'five minutes' had turned to 60.

The next day Goko's real brother came to see her.

'Suppose Goko did not commit this crime.'

'It's no good,' she told him. 'He's been found guilty in court.'

'Suppose I could produce the man whose opium it was?'

'Forget it. It was a fair trial. Let him serve his sentence quietly.'

But the brother persisted until she agreed to seek a statement from the other man. After several days and nights waiting for the old man to finish his opium smoking, they managed to get a statement from him. This matched with Goko's statement. There were difficulties with solicitors and the law trying to get the evidence admitted in the appeal court. Eventually the other man was convicted – 'he beamed at his short sentence and became a Christian too.'

Goko went before the supreme court and his appeal was allowed. He was a free man. The clerks of the court were heard to say that it was obviously better to have Jesus than the best defence counsel on offer.

Just before the case was heard, Goko, in a legal blunder, was released on bail. On the day, some of his Walled City friends hired a double-decker bus to join him for the special occasion of his baptism in the sea.

Goko was heard to say, it would be worth the short reprieve in order to acknowledge Jesus publicly at his baptism, and give up the leadership of his Triad.

Twelve months later, Goko went to a restaurant alone. A rival Triad gang attacked him. He put up his arms in defence against a chopper aimed for his head. His hand and arm were partially severed. He said later that he was really glad that it had happened to prove to doubters that he didn't want to fight any more. Despite his considerable pain, he took the unique step of forbidding his followers to avenge him.

When he was in hospital, just before the operation to try and save the use of his hand, the surgeon heard Goko apparently talking to himself, and asked him what he was saying. Goko told him he was praying to forgive his attackers and for the surgeon to do a good job. More than a little surprised, knowing full well who Goko was, the surgeon replied that he would do his very best. Goko, known today among friends as New Paul, now has the full use of both his hands.

Many people from all walks of life have been attracted to Jackie Pullinger's outreach opportunities to the poor and unloved.

Elizabeth, a doctor of science, joined the street sleepers team under the Kowloon City flyover during Chinese New Year 1986. She recalled:

As three of us gave a rice box to one man we asked if
we could pray for him and he agreed. He became very
still and peaceful, we continued to pray quietly. After
what seemed ages he opened his eyes and asked, 'Do
you know someone called Jesus?' to which we replied,
'Why?' 'Well I had this vision as you were praying. A
man dressed in white came to me and asked to be my
friend. I told him I had no friends and didn't know
how to be a friend. He said not to worry, he would
teach me if I wanted to be his friend. I answered that I
would like a friend but I wasn't used to having one.
He said: "First hold my hand and we will walk together in life, then later we will talk together".'

That's OK, have a good cry. Isn't it a touching story?

I just had to include the following story to encourage all those readers who are waiting on much peti-
tioned finances. This has strengthened me many
times when praying for funds for China trips and
has made me chuckle when I needed to.

Selling Cattle

Shortly after [Dallas] Seminary was founded in 1924, it
almost folded. It came to the point of bankruptcy. All
the creditors were ready to foreclose at twelve noon on
a particular day. That morning, the founders of the
school met in the president's office to pray that God

would provide. In that prayer meeting was Harry Ironside. When it was his turn to pray, he said in his refreshingly candid way, 'Lord, we know that the cattle on a thousand hills are Thine. Please sell some of them and send us the money.' Just about that time, a tall Texan in boots and an open-collared shirt strolled into the business office. 'Howdy!' he said to the secretary. 'I just sold two carloads of cattle over in Fort Worth. I've been trying to make a business deal go through, but it just won't work. I feel God wants me to give this money to the seminary. I don't know if you need it or not, but here's the check,' and he handed it over. The secretary took the check and, knowing something of the critical nature of the hour, went to the door of the prayer meeting and timidly tapped. Dr Lewis Sperry Chafer, the founder and president of the school, answered the door and took the check from her hand. When he looked at the amount, it was for the exact sum of the debt. Then he recognized the name on the check as that of the cattleman. Turning to Dr Ironside, he said, 'Harry, God sold the cattle.'[10]

One of our team members was praying for money for a China trip. 'My Father owns the cattle on a thousand hills, so He will provide,' was the bold statement she kept telling me whenever we talked about finances. It was a big ask – to pay for herself and her daughter to go to China when her husband, the only breadwinner, had just started his own business. There was another son in the family still at school. The Lord didn't provide the money in any overtly miraculous way but he did bless the family business so much so that in the last few weeks before they left, there was enough money for both mother and daughter to go on the trip, plus some spending money.

God knows what he wants to do even before we have an inkling.

A person anonymously sent to the pastor of a little country church, a cheque with a note saying that the money was to go to the person who would do ministry in China. At the time there was no one in the church who fitted that bill. A while later a lad heard about our team and expressed a wish to go on our tour to China, so he received this financial help. I have heard of God providing after the missionary tells the church his/her intentions, but this was the first occasion I have heard of money coming in before the idea had entered anyone else's head!

'What do you want me to do about this situation, Lord?'

This must be one of the most challenging questions we could ever ask because if we are acting within God's will, then he will certainly tell us his masterplan. Our question is the response to his call and who knows what will happen?

Across the previous pages have marched many people who saw the desperate situations others were caught in, through his eyes of compassion. Such an encounter, as I've known in my own life, leaves an indelible mark on one's soul. The Lord's voice drawing us into his ideas is undeniable.

Though facing an uncertain future, which only promises difficulties along the way, acceptance of one's calling to that area of service is not to be taken lightly. The temptation to run away is ever present.

I thank God for the work of these people mentioned and the many others who similarly accepted their calling – the world is a better place for their contribution. What would the world have been like if all of them pulled down the blinds, hibernated in a safe cocoon behind the excuse: 'It's too big, I'm too small, I'm closing down until the problems go away.' Would there be, for example, a string of orphanages in India if Keith Greenwood had not accepted his calling?

What would the world now be like if all the people God has called into service denied he had called them and run away? If Satan had achieved his goal, instead of our benevolent God? It's a horrific thought we don't wish to contemplate.

It is too glib an answer to assume if God calls a person who doesn't embrace the challenge, then he'll just call someone else. How infinitely disappointed Father God must feel after decades of nurturing the person for the area of mission when he/she runs away out of fear.

What celebrations in heaven there must be when one courageous servant accepts the hazardous venture and asks: 'What do you want me to do, Lord?' What would the celebrations in heaven be like when the servant later achieves the goals in the ministry and all the people they were asked to reach have been blessed? The planet's 2000 celebrations would pale into insignificance by comparison.

Following the example of the saints, my prayer for my readers is to be courageous the next time the Lord calls them into a demanding ministry. They will experience fulfilment and satisfaction unrivalled by anything the cocoon could ever offer. Oh yes, as our heroes have already taught us, there will be difficulties, pressures, misunderstandings, etc. – it's all part of the process!

Look at Jesus' opposition.

Look at what he achieved when he pressed on.

Living a radical lifestyle guided by the Lord rather than the world, satisfies the deeper needs which the cocoon could never gratify.

There is nothing to compare with the joy of serving within one's calling. Dissatisfaction comes when we step outside that circle. Nor will we see the fullness of God's power acting in and through us. Caroline Chisholm would have been stunned when she realised that at one point in time, she had assisted 11,000 people!

I pray that we discern the evil times we live in, understand the training the Lord has provided and have the eyes to see the world as God sees it and like these past and present heroes say:

> *'What do you want me to do about this situation, Lord?'*

---

1 Borthwick, p. 44
2 Borthwick, p. 46
3 Mackay, B., p. 256
4 Yancey, pp. 18, 21
5 Russell, p. 80

6   Perry, J., Heart Records, 1992
7   Pullinger, pp. 27
8   Pullinger, pp. 28–9
9   Pullinger, p. 83, 117
10 Hendricks, H., quoted in Gray, p. 279

Bibliography

Atkins, M., 'Ken Duncan: Images of Life', *Alive Magazine*, February 2000

Blanch, K., 'Rev John Flynn' in *100 Famous Lives*

Borthwick, P., *A Mind for Missions* (Colorado Springs: NavPress 1987)

Brabazon, J., *Albert Schweitzer: A Biography* (London: Victor Gollancz Ltd 1976)

Brown, R., 'Obituary: Peter King, Rural Surgeon', *The Age*, 24 December 1998

Carey, T., 'Obituary: Surgeon Urged Motorists to Belt up', *The Australian*, 5 January 1999

Clark, M., *History of Australia* (Carlton South: Melbourne University Press 1998)

Costello T., *Streets of Hope* (Sydney: Albatross Books 1998)

Cunningham, L. and Rogers, J., *Winning God's Way* (Seattle: Frontline Communications 1988)

Dalrymple, W., *In Xanadu: A Quest* (London: Collins 1989)

Dunlop, E. E., *The War Diaries of Weary Dunlop: Java and the Burma-Thailand Railway 1942–1945* (Melbourne: Thomas Nelson Australia 1986)

Este, J., 'Man who Chalked up an Eternal Legacy', *Weekend Australian*, 2 January 2000

Fetherston, G., *100 Famous Australian Lives*

Fletcher, M., 'Raising the Titanic: New Millennium Church', *Directions* 1999

Flynn, R., *Caroline Chisholm: The Emigrant's Friend* (South Melbourne: the Macmillan Co. of Aust. Pty Ltd 1991)

Gardiner, P. SJ., *An Extraordinary Australian: Mary MacKillop* (Newtown Sydney: E.J. Dwyer/David Ell Press 1993)

Gire, K., *Windows of the Soul* (Grand Rapids: Zondervan Publishing House 1996)

Gray, A., *Stories for the Heart* (Sisters: Multnomah Books 1996)

Grey, J., *A Military History of Australia* (Melbourne: University of Cambridge Press 1990)

Griffiths, M., *The Silent Heart: Flynn of the Inland* (Kenhurst: Kangaroo Press Pty Ltd 1993)

Grubb, N., *Rees Howells: Intercessor* (Lutterworth Press 1952/Fort Washington: Christian Literature Crusade 1993)

Hughes, E. S. R., 'Report to Council on the Activities of the Road Trauma Committee 1970-1975'

Hughes, E. S. R., MacLeish, D.G., Waterhouse, A.R., and Clareborough, J.K., *Proceedings of the First Seminar: The Management of Road Traffic Casualties* (The Royal Australasian College of Surgeons October 1969)

Hutchinson, G., *An Australian Odyssey: From Gaza to Gallipoli* (Sydney: Sceptre 1997)

Idress, I. L., *Flynn of the Inland* (Sydney: Angus & Robertson 1956 16th Ed.)

Inserra, R., *Mary MacKillop: Holy Mother to the Poor* (Carlton Melbourne: Cardigan Street 1995)

Jackman, W., *Life Stories: Mother Theresa* (Hove England: Wayland Ltd 1993)

Kempton, G., *The Passionate Edge* (Nashville: Broadman & Holman Publishers 1995)

Kenneally, T., Adam-Smith, P. and Davidson, R., *Australia: Beyond the Dreamtime* (Richmond Melbourne: William Heinemann Australia 1987)

Kiddle, M., *Caroline Chisholm,* (Carlton, Melbourne: Melbourne University Press 1990)

King, P., *Proceedings of the First Seminar 'The Management of Road Traffic Casualties'* conducted by The Royal Australasian College of Surgeons, October 1969,

Lasker, M., 'Peter Spitzer: Dr Fruitloop Helps Children Laugh in the face of Death', *The Australian Magazine,* 22–23 January 2000

Lemke, A. B., (translator) *Out of my Life and Thought: An Autobiography* by Albert Schweitzer (New York: Henry Holt & Co. Inc. 1990)

Lennon, T., 'Here's to Eternity', *The Daily Telegraph,* 24 December 1999

McGovern, D., 'A Word for all Eternity', *Alive Magazine,* 2, 2000

Mackay, B., *China's Dancer* (Carlisle: Paternoster 1999)

MacNeil, P. Dr and Gunn, I. Dr, *Peter King Obituary*

McPheat, W. S., *John Flynn: Apostle to the Inland* (London: Hodder & Stoughton Ltd 1963)

Maroun, M., 'Through Different Eyes', *Alive Magazine,* May 2000

Mesiti, P., *Wake up and Dream* (Castle Hill: Pat Mesiti Ministries 1994)

Monneret, S., translated by Dr L. Wildt, *Dürer* (London: Ferndale Editions 1980)

Nagle, J.F., *Collins, the Courts and the Colony*, (University of NSW Press 1996)

O'Brien, L., *Mary Mackillop Unveiled*, (Melbourne: CollinsDove 1994)

Patten, C., *East and West* (London: Macmillan Publishers Ltd 1998)

Peach, K., Pub. Co-ord., *The Asialink Centre 1995–1997* (The Asialink Centre: Melbourne 1997)

Pollard, M., *Pioneers in History: People who Care* (Oxford: Heinemann Educational Books Ltd 1991)

Pollard, M., *The Red Cross and the Red Crescent* (Watford: Exley Publications Ltd 1992)

Pullinger, J. and Quicke, A., *Chasing the Dragon* (London: Hodder & Stoughton 1980)

Pullinger, J., *Crack in the Wall: Life and Death in Kowloon Walled City* (Sevenoaks: Hodder & Stoughton 1989)

Robles, H. E., *Albert Schweitzer: An Adventurer for Humanity* (Brookfield: The Millbrook Press 1994)

Ross, Pastor R., 'Humble Message Echoes Eternal', *The Citizen*, 3 January 2000

Rundall, C., vol. ed., *Across the Outback* (Surry Hills: Reader's Digest Association Ltd 1996)

Russell, A.J., *God Calling* (Geebung: W.A. Buchanan & Co., 1997 24th edn)

Senter, R., 'One brave missionary did not look back even in the face of great personal loss', *Christian Reader*, vol. 36 no. 4 (1998)

Shreve, M., *Our Glorious Inheritance: The Revelation of the Titles of the Children of God* (Cleveland: Deeper Revelation Books 1991, vol. 6)

Smith, L., 'Canvassing Ancient Symbols', *Alive Magazine*, February 2000

The Official Mackillop Papal Visit Book 1995, (Pymble: Playbill Proprietary Ltd 1995)

The Sir Edward Weary Dunlop Asia Awards, pamphlet (Asialink: Melbourne)

Theresa, Mother, 'Carriers of Christ's Love', *A Gift for God* (1975)

Thomas, B., 'Ten Great Australian Christians', *New Life Christian Newspaper*, 20 January 2000

Various editors, *100 Famous Australian Lives* (Paul Hamlyn P/L: Sydney, 1969)

Wellman, S., *Mother Theresa: Missionary of Charity* (Uhrichsville: Barbour Inc 1997)

Wilson, G., *The Flying Doctor Story: Authorised History of the Royal Flying Doctor Service of Australia* (Glen Waverley: Cyan Press Pty Ltd 1993)

Yancey, P., *What's so Amazing About Grace?* (Grand Rapids: Zondervan Publishing House 1997)

Yancey, P., *Where is God when it Hurts?* (Grand Rapids: Zondervan Publishing House 1990)

Ma Ma Hta

Denise Macdonald

1-85078-372-1

The startling account of a headwoman over
200 families who, while living in occupied
Burma in the 1940s, was branded as a
traitor and a British sympathiser. As
the story shows the Japanese Imperial
Army sweeping across South East Asia, a
beautiful world unknown to many
Westerners comes alive through stories of
human struggle, desperation and humility.

OM
publishing

Fire Within

Woo Yung

1-85078-355-1

In this moving autobiography of Wu Yung, leader of the church in Taiwan, his personal experiences of faith in God provide the reader with valuable insights into effective church witness and itinerant world-wide ministry.

OM
publishing

A New Chapter

The Mick Whitburn Story
Retold by Jill Gupta

1-85078-373-X

For 26 years Mick Whitburn led a life dominated by crime, drugs and violence. His habitual response to anything or anybody was sarcastic, critical and cold. A former Hell's Angel and estranged from his family, he drifted from one encounter with the law to the next. Now his life has been transformed by a faith in Jesus, though this did not happen overnight. He is still in and out of prison, but now it's as a volunteer leading Alpha groups and prayer meetings. Today Mick works on the streets as a seller of the 'Big Issue' and preacher of the Gospel.

OM
publishing

You Will See Hoopoes

Lenna Lidstone

1-85078-370-5

Looking at mission at the turn of the 21st Century, this is the story of church planting in Turkey, probably the largest un-evangelised country in the world. It tells of the author's experiences and the lessons she learned from the special acts of God's grace and the wonders of his love.

OM
publishing

Serving as Senders

Neal Pirolo

1-85078-199-0

'This key book makes the point that mobilizers - the senders - are as crucial to the cause of missions as frontline missionaries. It is a book just crammed with solid, exciting insights on the most hurting link in today's mission movement.'

Ralph Winter
US Centre for World Mission

'Unless the Church and God's people respond to this book's message, the work of reaching the unreached is going to be greatly hindered. Every committed sender needs to get involved in distributing this book.'

George Verwer, *Operation Mobilisation*

Neal Pirolo is the founding Director of Emmaus Road International, San Diego, California, mobilizing churches, training cross-cultural teams and networking fellowships with national ministries around the world.

OM
publishing